ANTONI GAUDÍ

ANTONI GAUDÍ

IGNASI DE SOLÀ-MORALES

PHOTOGRAPHS BY RAFAEL VARGAS

HARRY N. ABRAMS, INC., PUBLISHERS

We wish to express our thanks to the Gaudí Chair of the Higher Technical School of Architecture of Barcelona for the cooperation given in obtaining the graphic and documentary material for this book.

Text first published in Ignasi de Solà-Morales: *Gaudí*, Ed. Polígrafa, Barcelona, 1983.

This edition © 2003 Ediciones Polígrafa, S. A.
Balmes, 54 - 08007 Barcelona
www.edicionespoligrafa.com

Text © Eulàlia Serra de Budallès
Photographs © Rafael Vargas

Coordination: Montse Holgado
Translation: Kenneth Lyons
Copy editing: Rafael Galisteo, Sue Brownbridge
Design: Estudi Polígrafa / B. Martínez
Jacket design, English-language edition: Michael J. Walsh Jr.
Production: Rafael Aranda
Color separation: Format Digital, Barcelona
Printing: Mateu Cromo, Madrid
Dep. legal: B. 20.510 - 2003

Library of Congress Cataloging-in-Publication Data
Solà-Morales Rubio, Ignasi, 1942-
[Gaudí. English]
Antoni Gaudí / Ignasi Solà-Morales ; photography by Rafael Vargas.
    p. cm.
Includes bibliographical references and index.
ISBN 0–8109–4625–4 (alk. paper)
1. Gaudí, Antoni, 1852–1926—Criticism and interpretation. 2.
Eclecticism in architecture—Spain—Catalonia. I. Vargas, Rafael, 1959–
II. Title.
NA1313.G3S6413 2003
720'.92—dc21
2003007534

CONTENTS

AN ARCHITECTURE FOR A CITY

The architectural work of Gaudí is inseparable from Barcelona. Although not all of his great works were built in this city, it is certainly a fact that his total *œuvre* cannot be understood unless we establish a direct relationship with all the aspirations and transformations that affected the city between the last quarter of the 19th century and the second decade of the 20th.

Architecture is never a phenomenon enclosed in itself but a social manifestation. The form and language of this manifestation are inseparable from the objectives and aspirations that prevail at certain levels of the class, or classes, in power at a given moment in history. But this does not come about by chance, nor even as the result of a direct connection between the ideas collectively dominating a particular historical period and the physical shape of that period's architectural objects, for any such connection is mediated by the urban surroundings in which the architecture is actually built. Thus the first explicative relationship that we must establish in order to understand the work of Gaudí is undoubtedly that between this work and the city in which it was produced, with an analysis, at the same time, of the circumstances of the city in Gaudí's day and the explanation of these circumstances that we can find in architecture as the plastic language of urban space.

Throughout the 19th century Barcelona was constantly expanding. With the pulling down of the old city walls in 1854 and, later, the laying out of the "Extension Plan" proposed by Ildefons Cerdà, the municipal area grew from less than twenty hectares to a potential of over two hundred. The driving forces behind this expansion were the cotton, iron and steel industries, whose need for workers produced a steady flow of immigration. Between 1850 and 1900 the population quadrupled, rising from 150,000 inhabitants to 600,000, who occupied the historic central area of the city and, at a rapidly increasing rate, the new buildings in the original "Plain" of Barcelona, now laid out in the grid pattern established in the Extension Plan (the Eixample).

The industries, moreover, were also moving their factories from their original locations on the outskirts of the walled city to some of the nearby villages, thus creating a rough circle of industrial districts beyond the limits of the Eixample — the use of which for industry was never more than secondary. In this way districts or villages like Sants, Sant Andreu, Gràcia and Barceloneta formed the new periphery of an urban structure of a very dynamic kind that still had to be formed in each and every one of its elements.

This new city, which the people of 19th-century Barcelona saw growing at such a tremendous rate, had to reappraise its more important services, its monuments, and its most representative public buildings in order to conform to the idea of a city that was definitively taking on the characteristics of a great metropolitan center.

Really, however, the urban development of Barcelona is simply the most concentrated — and therefore the most visible — aspect in the process of the transformation of a whole region. When Pierre Vilar speaks pf the transformation in the region of Barcelona, he is also referring to that of all the nearby areas, which were completely drawn into the same process; and the consequence of this process, in the fields of transport, energy and trade, was to be the foundation of a metropolitan area eager to share, as regards both town planning and culture, in the same adventure of modernity.

The transformations involved in Barcelona's development into a metropolis also affected the form of its principal historic districts. The port, the old fortress of the Ciutadella, the very fabric of the historic city, had to adapt to the new metropolitan scale being assumed by the modern town. The process included great changes in the relationship between the city and its port, the laying out of the first large-scale municipal park, and the opening of great new streets, their width and straightness ensuring faster traffic, through the old maze of medieval lanes and alleys that had hitherto been enclosed by the city walls. I am making all these references because these were the sites, the spaces old and new, on which Gaudí was to work and in the characterization of which he was to insert his own conception of architecture, his own contribution to the formation of the backdrop, so to speak, against which the new metropolitan life was to be lived. But the new city, too, was to be an architectural problem. Both the districts that grew up in the vast network of the Cerdà Eixample and the more distant areas that formed the industrial ring around Barcelona proper, and awaited their turn in the incessant enlargement brought about by the growing population, were to contain examples of Gaudí's architecture. Blocks of flats, detached houses for gentlemen, churches and schools, housing estates for workers and new garden suburbs: these were some of the things the new metropolis needed. And Gaudí, far from eluding the problems they presented, always endeavored to solve them in the way best suited to the new urban concepts and demands.

The Barcelona of that time, rapidly becoming one of the most important metropolitan areas in the Mediterranean world, was marked by a profoundly felt optimism. The newly ascendant industrial bourgeoisie had consolidated their power in Catalonia after the restoration of the constitutional monarchy in 1874 and the end of the civil wars in 1876. Catalonia's essential difference from the rest of the Spanish state lay at the root of the tensions between Catalan nationalism and desire for autonomy on the one hand, and the reformism of the state as a whole on the other. The metropolitan expansion that was the setting for Gaudí's work was in itself a political project. It was an attempt to give shape to the image of a new class, that of the industrial entrepreneurs who, in their newfound social predominance, wanted to endow the city with a form and an architectural image that would reflect their ability to transform the relationships between production and the social structure, and the space in which those relationships and that structure existed. The optimism of the members of this new class, with their faith in economic progress and in the capacity of reason to cope with the new situations, showed itself in the efforts made to give material form to their aspirations through a veritable explosion of creative activities. The artists were called upon to provide a tangible fulfillment of those aspirations and to expound the characteristics of the new social order in a comprehensible fashion. The role of art and architecture, like those of other cultural activities, was to be quite clearly linked to these ideas. A contribution to the new age, to this new period of wealth and welfare, progress and expansion, was the most profound ideal for which the new ruling class wanted its artists and intellectuals to work.

Pablo Picasso: *Charity,* c. 1899. Drawing on paper, 22.9 x 33.5 cm. Picasso Museum, Barcelona.

But this general picture of optimism in the creation of a new social order was not in fact reflected, on the part of the artists, by an equally optimistic and harmonious response demonstrating their unlimited confidence in the future. On the contrary, indeed, both in the architecture of Gaudí and in other manifestations of the restoration period, the forward-looking optimism that characterized the culture of this 19th-century industrial bourgeoisie was tempered by a critical conscience that was just as incisive and radical.

The period of Catalan culture during which Gaudí's work was produced was that of the movement known in Catalonia as *Modernisme,* which was more or less the local name for Art Nouveau. As was the case in other great cities of Europe — Paris, Vienna, Brussels, Milan, Glasgow, etc. — the *Modernisme* of Catalonia really represented, both in the field of literature and in that of the plastic arts, a general loss of confidence in 19th-century cultural models and an attempt by artists to express themselves in a language that would be at once genuine and elitist in relation to society as a whole.

Modernisme always had a strong tinge of Catalan nationalism, and its roots were supposed to lie in a native tradition, which some Catalans were now trying to revive. In this seems to reside its first problem: that of its cultural identity. As against the indiscriminate consumption of the universal culture of all ages that was preached by the progressive elements, *Modernisme* endeavored to express specific characteristics of its own — the sort of manners, traditions or "spirit of place" that did not contriibute to the universalism of the imperialistic capitalism of the time but, on the contrary, sought to go more deeply into everything local and vernacular, thus expressing these artists' criticism of the uniformity inevitably established by an industrial civilization.

Thus, the problem of tradition in *Modernisme* — and in Gaudí — sounds the first note of criticism of the industrial bourgeoisie's thrusting optimism. It established a more complex, dialectical relationship between tradition and innovation, introducing a mediating element between absolute novelty and change on the one hand, and sheer reactionary immobility on the other.

Another aspect that should not be neglected is that of the *Modernista* view of society. The great new metropolis did not develop as a harmonious whole, but was in fact plagued with contradictions and dysfunctions that can be detected and visualized in the more negative aspects of the industrial world. There was, in the first place, what today we might call the fringe society. Alongside the dazzling new splendor of the great cities — Barcelona among them — there was often dreadful poverty. At this time, indeed, the poor, the fringe dwellers, the frightful slums, dirt and unhygienic conditions, disease and loneliness all went to make up a phenomenon of increasing proportions. The paintings of Nonell, or those of Picasso's Barcelona period, dealt with the life of the fringe society, not gratuitously but as the artists' response to a real and disquieting aspect of the developing metropolitan society. In Gaudí, too, the problems of the misfits and the poor were subjects that were to be expressed more and more in his work through his stylization of the elemental and the way he resorted to poor, coarse materials in his externalization of the anguished compassion that moved the intellectuals of the period. It is true, of course, that at first glance *Modernisme,* like parallel movements in other European cities, will seem to be almost exclusively an explosion of splendor and luxury, a wealth of decoration, a sumptuous and flagrant display of ornamentation. Yet both the ornamental motifs in the applied arts and the brilliant, exuberant use of color in painting did not simply reflect the confident enthusiasm of the new ruling class but also revealed a pure, agonizing insecurity and an explicit fragility.

Any relationship with nature had become difficult and remote, while the dynamism of the urban world was chaotic in its constant change. All security and order seemed to have vanished, giving way instead to an aggressive, competitive atmosphere, in which no amount of decorative magnificence could conceal the disturbing presence of the uncontrollable, the irrational, and the contradictory.

It was surely not by pure chance that the art of the *Modernista* period was so favorably reexamined by the Surrealists, who saw in it an early expression of their own dissatisfaction, their own critical stance regarding the gay, overconfident culture of the bourgeoisie.

In the case of Gaudí this critical and insecure attitude crystallized, as his work became more mature, into the religious and social utopianism of a Catholic faith that was militantly reformist in its attitude toward contemporary metropolitan life. He gradually came to be more and more closely associated with the circle of thinkers and social reformers who, inspired by a renewed Catholic doctrine, tenaciously attempted, from within the system itself, to put a moderately critical curb on the optimism of 19th-century progressivism. Since he was inclined to be pessimistic about the human condition, and came to reveal increasingly redemptionist intentions in his art, in the context of *Modernista* culture Gaudí's work exemplified an attitude that was in fact both critical and significant in respect to the more properly aestheticist positions typical of the European culture of the day. The expressionist roots discerned in Gaudí by the members of the German *Frühlicht* movement or the Dutch *Wendingen* in the second decade of the 20th century was a correct interpretation of the critical tension that made Gaudí in some ways a peripheral figure in relation to *Modernisme* as a whole, a figure characterized by a conception at once more complex and more contradictory than that of most artists of his generation. Not only because in Gaudí the model of boundless, continuous progress is opposed by the summons to tradition, but also because his work counters the new ethic of productive, conquering freedom with a defense of the preindustrial organic order to the benefit of the principle of authority, the traditional social structure and the educative and moralizing character of art.

THE SITUATION IN EUROPEAN ARCHITECTURE

The obsession of the most clear-sighted architects in 19th-century Europe was the search for their own identity. The question "In what style should we construct the buildings of our age?" can be found over and over again in texts, treatises and the records of professional meetings, synthesizing the polemics aroused by the great changes inherent in contemporary industrial society.

This civilization had introduced a positive method for facing most questions: in dealing with any problem, one endeavored to consider all such results as past experience might offer, and then to

Eugène Emmanuel Viollet-le-Duc: Construction in stone and cast iron. *Entretiens sur l'architecture,* Plate XXIII. Paris, 1864.

H. P. Berlage: Stock Exchange, Amsterdam.
Contracting hall. 1903.

arrange and analyze them in such a way as to obtain some solid, convincing knowledge from the operation. This, of course, was also the rule in architecture, for 19th-century architectural culture was of a positive nature. The authority of the classics was no longer accepted as indisputable doctrine, and from an empirical knowledge of the architecture of the past it could be shown that the architectural problems that had arisen through the centuries had been solved in very different ways. This meant that as a result of this research, contemporary architecture seemed to be lost in a sea of doubts. Why was Greek architecture better than Muslim? Why had we followed the Renaissance-Classical tradition, forgetting all the positive aspects of medieval architecture? What were the comparative advantages of one or the other? What were the aspects that should be given priority when it came to choosing a solution based on the past: the constructive, the economic, the symbolic? These were some of the questions that constantly beset the architects of the 19th century; and it was exactly this type of problem, as we shall see, that Gaudí had to cope with.

European architecture at first found only one answer, which was that of eclecticism. There was no previous judgment that could determine the priority of any given historical tradition over another, nor could any absolute criterion decide what the style of the future should be — if it was to be supposed that any such style would be simply the continuation of one of the many styles of the past.

In any event, this eclectic culture, which had all past styles, all traditions, without limit at its disposal, established the first prerequisites for renewal and for the invention of an absolutely new style — which was at all times the ultimate aspiration of the architects of the day. They may not have known what this new way of giving shape to architecture would be like, but they did know that it could not consist in simply prolonging the results of the past. In establishing the inviability of any mere exploitation of tradition and history, the eclectic culture likewise established the need to transcend the traditions, mingling all their teachings afresh in a single crucible, from which would emerge the language of the new age — their own positive, scientific and industrial age.

Among all the experiments and proposals aimed at doing away with eclectic architecture, and with that aftertaste of Neoclassicism that was at bottom the real center of that style, undoubtedly the strongest movement of all was the one that reappraised the possibilities offered by medieval architecture — particularly Gothic architecture. In France, England, Germany and Italy, as well as Spain, there was a powerful tendency that led architects to approach Gothic architecture with the conviction that in it were to be found the most satisfying teachings for solving the problems of contemporary architects.

Gothic architecture was seen above all else as the opposite of the classicist tradition. While the classical architects, from Brunelleschi to Quatremère de Quincy, had viewed Gothic architecture with horror as a veritable sample-book of incongruencies, now, since the chief desire among many others was to demolish the smug security of the classicists, this view had to be diametrically reversed; that is to say, things had to be seen from the point of view of that architectural system with which the classicists had declared their utter incompatibility.

Hector Guimard: Canopy over the entrance to the Paris
Metro. 1900.

But the vindication of Gothic also had moral and even political connotations. Gothic was the
style of European spirituality, which meant the recovery for architecture of a certain dimension
of the sublime. Gothic architecture was an architecture with immediate roots in the religious and
transcendental, and it was through these references that modern architecture might rediscover the
lost values of its artistic feeling.

Pugin, for instance, believed that the only antidote architecture could provide for the materialism
and spiritual impoverishment of modern man was that of its spirituality. Architecture, since it was a
collective task, appeared to him as the manifestation of a social order that had existed in the past
and should now be restored.

On the one hand there was the idea of a collective, anonymous achievement, the result of
collaboration by different craftsmen, each one with his own particular skill and knowledge,
and this seemed to reinvent for architecture its character as a place for cooperation and honest,
painstaking work.

The work of art could be thought of as a task to which each man contributed his particular skill and
effort, one in which nobody set himself up as a solitary genius or a definitive authority. These ideals
of work and collaboration were those of social reformism; and they were also the expression, in the
context of art and architecture, of more profound aspirations that came from the architects' own
view of society and from their critical attitude toward the contemporary situation. This way of
evaluating architectural work was clearly shared by Gaudí.

On the other hand, however, Gothic architecture also meant the reinforcement of the ideals of
national cultures, so much more individual and authentic than the indiscriminate internationalism
of the classicist language still maintained by the eclectic tradition.

Apart from the decline and fall of the *ancien régime,* the principal political feature of the 19th
century in Europe was the formation of nation states. This formation, however, was not merely
an affair of constitutions or geographical frontiers, but was also determined by linguistic, cultural
and artistic peculiarities. In this sense Gothic art, and the medieval structural and stylistic traditions
in general, may be seen as the source of differential positions. English Gothic, for instance, is a very
different thing from the Gothic of northern Italy or southern Germany. For the social and cultural
aspirations that characterized the nationalisms of the period, the restoration of this element of
identity in contemporary art meant the possession of something that would identify the political
project with the artistic results and with the very construction of the state. The interest aroused
in 19th-century Catalonia by the country's own traditions — the local Gothic and the technical and
stylistic solutions that characterized it — was directly linked to that aspiration to a national identity
that was fostered by the metropolitan culture of Barcelona. The Catalan character of Gaudí's
architecture was emphasized from the very moment it first appeared, either by the architect
himself or by the collaborators, critics and politicians who saw in it an evident example of how the
originality of his work should be associated with the search for the vernacular and autochthonous in
all fields of cultural creative activity.

Gaudí's work, however, also shared other yearnings characteristic of the European architecture of his time, yearnings that had their origin not so much in nationalistic or religious feelings as in his contemporaries' trust in the science and technology of their age as reliable guides in a search for the most suitable solutions to the problems of the day.

This insistence on finding the architecture best suited to the needs and resources of the new society meant that architects had to apply themselves to the critical study of the procedures used by the architectures of the past. A rationalistic attitude toward the teachings of the past required that they be subject to criticism and, above all, reappraisal in light of the more precise knowledge that was now available in the fields of archaeology, history and the study of the resistance of materials and the statics of buildings.

The great master of this attitude was undoubtedly Eugène Emmanuel Viollet-le-Duc, an architect apparently devoted to archaeology and restoration, but one who made his studies of medieval French architecture a permanent reflection on the general problems of the architecture of his time.

He attempted to make a rational analysis of the way in which the different solutions actually worked in building, evaluating their safety and efficacy, as also the suitability of the materials employed to the form of the building; he set himself the problem of the building's final form and appearance, as in the result of the technical methods used in its construction: these were the basic preoccupations dealt with in this French architect's copious publications, which very soon found their way all over Europe and became quite familiar to Catalan architects in the closing years of the 19th century.

For Viollet-le-Duc the only way of arriving at a genuine architecture for his time was by advancing along the road of constructive rationality, from the choice of material to the particular solution of every technical detail. Beyond the forms offered by the past, this position represents a decided attitude toward tradition that is assured by its own stock of technical and scientific knowledge. With the conviction that the methods used in the past for measuring the efficiency and exactitude of building had been vastly inferior to those available in their own time, the men who maintained this attitude were not afraid to manipulate the different traditions, reconsidering them and modifying them to whatever extent they found suitable for the sake of perfection; in order to achieve this, they put their faith in technical rationality as the ultimate justification of architectural form.

The fact that for Viollet-le-Duc in particular — as also for his disciple, Gaudí — it was from Gothic that 19th-century architecture had the greatest lessons to learn simply means that the reasons I have already mentioned (those concerning the interest aroused by Gaudí's architecture) were now reinforced by more timeless, and more purely rational, reasons, through which these architects believed that it was possible to go beyond eclecticism and arrive at an architecture at once more authentic and better suited to the new era. For the architecture of modern times, Viollet-le-Duc means the establishment of critical and interpretive freedom with regard to the past. The various historical styles could no longer be seen as definitively closed and labeled repertoires, regarding which the only possible option was to adopt them or to leave them. This rational approach, on the contrary, implied the assurance of believing that by applying the critical faculties to the technical, constructive and statical reasons behind what was already built, a sure road would be opened for the invention of the new architecture for which everybody was clamoring.

Gaudí, who never concealed his admiration for the ideas and studies developed by Viollet-le-Duc, and who is known to have possessed all the latter's most important works, was only one among many architects powerfully influenced by his way of thinking. Gaudí was more radical in some aspects, above all in the redesigning of the supporting structures of buildings, more traditional in others — for instance, in the limited use he made of the new materials and of the consequences deriving from those materials in the final form of the building. Nevertheless, the work of the Catalan master should not be seen as an isolated phenomenon, but as a variant of an overall process and one that is paralleled in other great European figures.

H. P. Berlage (1856–1934) in Amsterdam, Victor Horta (1861–1947) in Brussels, and Anatole de Baudot (1834–1915) and Hector Guimard (1867–1942) in Paris were also direct followers of the teachings of Viollet-le-Duc, and in all of them we find this freer approach to the design of the supporting structure of buildings and, consequently, to those buildings' ultimate shape.

In all of them we seem to detect, from the start, a habit of reflecting on the Gothic construction system advocated by Viollet-le-Duc, the idea of an autonomous system in which the coherence between the form of the supporting structure and the final form of the building seems to be the most important subject. To isolate the structural, designing it with a view to its utmost suitability to its material and to the requirements of stability, would appear to be the imperfect lesson that Gothic was to teach all of these men, the lesson that they were to take to more precise and refined stages, whether by using new materials — especially in the cases of Horta and Guimard, with their steel structures, or in the case of de Baudot and his incipient structures in reinfroced concrete — or with traditional materials such as brick and stone, as in the case of Gaudí and, partially, Berlage.

The modifications they all initiated with regard to the stylistic codes established by historical architecture came from that same freedom to break away and redesign on the basis of a constructive and statical criticism of the solutions of the past. In all of them, too, there was the conviction that the progress of architecture was possible, and that it was made possible by way of technological rationality in building.

EARLY YEARS

Antoni Gaudí i Cornet was born in Reus (Tarragona) on June 25, 1852, and was the son of a boilermaker who came from a farming family established in the nearby village of Riudoms. The Gaudí family originally hailed from the Auvergne in the south of France and had emigrated to Catalonia in the 17th century, probably fleeing religious persecution.

The future architect was the youngest in a family of five, most of whom died young, and his childhood and adolescence were spent in Reus, where he had his secondary schooling at the

Project for a covered courtyard for the Provincial Council of Barcelona. Published by Ràfols in 1929. 1876.

Project for a covered courtyard for the Provincial Council of Barcelona. Detail in watercolor, scale 1:25. Archives of the E.T.S.A.B. 1876.

local *instituto*. His lively character and only fair-to-middling fondness for his school subjects were already evident in those early years. The marks he was given, both during his secondary education and later, when he was studying architecture, were not exactly those that denote a student who works carefully and systematically. On the contrary, his academic record reveals a determined character who devoted himself to what attracted him, nonchalantly ignoring anything that, for one reason or another, failed to arouse his interest. Familiar to us from those early years in Reus, moreover, is the plan he and his friend, Eduard Toda, formed for the restoration of the monastery of Poblet, at that time abandoned and in ruins. It was not simply that the buildings of the huge monastery excited a sort of excursionist's interest when they visited the place in the summer of 1867; they actually made enthusiastic plans for its restoration, not simply as an exercise in archaeology but with a view to revitalizing the monastery itself, envisaging a sort of industrial phalanstery within its precincts. During the final, lingering death throes of Romanticism in Catalonia, the ruins of Poblet were an almost inevitable element in the original vocation of the great architects of the period. Even before their careers began, Rogent, Domènech and Gaudí, among others, seem to have sought the encouragement of those noble medieval stones to persist in their vocation. One would say that the great Cistercian foundation, undoubtedly one of the most important works in the whole history of Catalonia, wove a peculiar sort of symbolic spell when it came to awakening the architectural vocations of those who wanted to produce a kind of architecture that would be at once universal and firmly rooted in its own native soil.

In 1873 Gaudí left his home for Barcelona and enrolled in the Provincial School of Architecture, where he was to find an atmosphere that, though indeed provincial, was also one of great enthusiasm, as exemplified in the roster of the first members of its faculty. The Barcelona School of Architecture was a very recent creation, having evolved out of the architecture class at the old Academy of Noble Arts. But in this latest phase its character was transformed by the special attention paid to the technological and professional training of architects. Hitherto there had been only one school of architecture in Spain, that of Madrid, and the new foundation in Barcelona was to be, from this moment and for many years, the second school of architecture in the country.

The character of the school was conferred on it by two unmistakable constituent elements. On the one hand, a great faith in the technological training of architects, probably as a reaction against the lack of training of this kind in the earlier schools attached to the Academy. On the other hand, the contemporary yearning to transcend eclecticism by means of a scholarly and universalist training. Behind the teaching of Rogent, Serrallac, Torras, Vilaseca, Font, Villar, Rovira, Domènech i Montaner, etc., we find very strong influences from the French and German schools; a vast amount of attention to historical culture, through all sorts of studies of the monuments of the past and their constructive, typological and ornamental possibilities. But we also find the very clear-sighted opinion that this historical culture was not an untouchable heritage but material available for design purposes that could and should be used in accordance with certain functional, economic and technical criteria. The eclectic climate of these men's teaching was not incompatible with the positivism of attitudes that placed scientific truth above any other criterion. Yet it is a well-known fact that Gaudí, as a

Project for final examinations. Assembly hall for a university. Archives of the E.T.S.A.B. Section in watercolor, scale 1:100. 1877.

Project for a cemetery gateway. Published by Ràfols in 1929. Destroyed in 1936.

Lantern on the railings of Ciutadella Park, carried out during the period when Gaudí was assistant to the Superintendent of Works, J. Fontserè. c. 1876.

student, was not particularly attached to the school and the circles of the more influential teachers. Neither his academic record there nor anything in his subsequent attitude toward the place gives us the idea of a student happily integrated into the prevailing scholastic discipline and order. On the contrary, he was always to think, in opposition to all book learning or academic teaching, that one should at all times favor direct experience, personal work and fidelity to one's own impulses above all the conventions of the scholars.

Of his designs as a student only a few are known, the most interesting of which are those of a covered central courtyard for a building intended for the Provincial Council, an entrance gateway to a cemetery and an assembly hall for a university. The first of these shows the technical meticulousness with which the designs were executed and the precision with which he designed the divisions of the stone arches and columns or the elements supporting the metal roof over the courtyard. The most outstanding feature of the second design is the freedom with which certain historical themes are reinterpreted in a large-scale monumental work. A magnificent arch, gently emphasized and with a bossed intrados very much in the classicist idiom, is incorporated in a massive gateway crowned by a free, stepped interpretation of Lombard-Romanesque arching, which on the sides is given a more orthodox form with the presence of buttresses dividing the surface of the wall. A huge double metal gate with a sloping brace, like those Gaudí was frequently to use throughout his professional career, was intended to close this Romantic gateway, which shows a greater concern for the effects of the sublime than for the coherence of the details.

The design for a university assembly hall, which was a work presented for his final examination, is really a complex assemblage of architectural details of the most widely varying provenance. On a hemispherical dome of classical cut, with a circular ambulatory of an Early Christian type, this design proposes a dazzling scheme of ornamentation, with elements of Mudéjar, Hispano-Moresque and Egyptian art, which seems to be the result of an accumulation of colorful, exotic details rather than the consequence of any clear, previously decided stylistic idea.

In any event, Gaudí's interest in the School of Architecture seems to be of secondary importance in comparison with the apprenticeship he served throughout his student years as an assistant in various architectural practices in Barcelona.

Since his family was far from affluent, in order to eke out the allowance they gave him during his years as a student, Gaudí had to work for a number of different architects, in buildings by whom it is sometimes possible to detect traces of his early style. At the same time he was providing himself with specific experience and developing that taste for practical problems that was to be a constant throughout his professional career.

He collaborated with Joan Martorell, for instance, during the years in which that architect was working on the Convent of the Order of the Visitation in Barcelona (1882) and on the design (never carried out) of a Benedictine monastery for Villaricos, in the province of Almería. The taste for both Gothic and Mudéjar art in Martorell's work had an intense appeal for

Lamppost for the Plaça Reial in Barcelona. 1878.

Gaudí, in whose earliest work as an independent architect this taste was to be revealed in very noticeable fashion.

Gaudí also worked for Francisco de Paula del Villar, a teacher at the school of architecture and an architect for the diocese of Barcelona. Paula del Villar was also the architect who first began the work on the church of the Sagrada Família, which Gaudí was later to continue for the rest of his life. Gaudí was likewise del Villar's assistant on a job entailing an historicist approach: the Neo-Romanesque apse for the basilica in the Monastery of Montserrat. But perhaps the most fruitful of these student assistantships, both in the diversity of the work to be done and in the degree of freedom Gaudí seems to have been given in doing it, was the one he had in the office of the master builder Josep Fontserè i Mestres.

Though Fontserè was not an officially qualified architect, in 1869 he was commissioned to transform the precincts of the old citadel of Barcelona into a municipal park (now the Ciutadella Park) and to redesign the surrounding area. The landscaping, the great monumental cascade-fountain, the buildings, railings, walls and monuments were all entrusted to Fontserè, and Gaudí's contribution to much of this work is both evident and important. In the design of the great cistern for the operation of the cascade, in some of the monumental sculptures, in the grilles and cast-iron gates at the park entrances, Gaudí left his mark — still that of a novice, tyro, but by no means lacking in force or, above all, imagination. Some constants in Gaudí's career, such as the inscriptions and the use of motifs from nature in the ornamentation, or of airy plumes and elaborate sculptural motifs in the design of grilles and lampposts, made their first appearance in the work he did for Fontserè. The lively curiosity that led him to make use of everything and to experiment with all sorts of solutions and motifs is, as it were, foreshadowed in all this work he did in his student years, in which scholarly precision and conventionality seem to be opposed to the specific taste for the material and for the craftsman's work that forms it, in a direct approach to the trades that construct architecture piece by piece.

Project for lighting for the Sea Wall in Barcelona. 1881.

Quite a few of the first commissions Gaudí had to cope with when he qualified as an architect in 1877 were also of this particular kind, entailing close attention to the specific conditions of their execution.

The lampposts Gaudí designed for Plaça Reial in Barcelona in 1878 and the more ambitious 1881 designs for lighting the Sea Wall, or the furniture he designed for himself, the display cabinets for the Cumella house or the shrines and altars he was commissioned to do during those early professional years are all prooducts of an accumulative arrangement of materials, symbols and design solutions.

From the very start of his career, too, we can see Gaudí's encyclopedic taste for using the most varied repertoires of symbols: those of classicism, those of medieval heraldry, those of ecclesiastical symbology, those of nature taken realistically in its plant or animal forms. All these cases are often accumulated in complex systems of discordant scales, creating a sort of multiple approach to the object designed. This can be seen as a whole in the hierarchy of the principal components, but it

Interior for the industrial plant of the Workers' Cooperative of Mataró, with convex wooden frames forming parabolic arches. Mataró, Barcelona. 1883.

can also be seen in the particular order of one or another of its parts and in the subdivision established by ornaments and adjuncts in a vast system of complex relationships. There is, of course, a certain degree of the *horror vacui* peculiar to the period — the Victorian passion for superimposing and multiplying motifs and techniques. But there is also a sensibility in which the macrocosmic and the microcosmic meet, which in any of the objects designed by him arouses an inexhaustible sensation of dilation and infinity produced by the endless mechanism of subdivision and hierarchy that is a constant in his work.

This whole complex world of forms, however, is neither gratuitous nor blandly reiterative, but always has a sound, tightknit formal structure, whether in the statical problems of support in furniture, altars or lampposts, in changes of materials or in the technical solutions of joining, soldering or dovetailing. In all those works he took considerable care not to conceal any irregularities of the design but to show quite openly the process of the piece's construction or assembly.

The graceful lampposts designed by Gaudí for the Sea Wall, with their height of twenty meters and their rich vocabulary of symbols and allusions, or the wooden architecture of the prie-dieu for the Marqués de Comillas' chapel — a heavy Gothic bracket on slender column shafts — are among the many other works that show the young architect's boundless symbolic and constructive imagination.

Among these early works I should perhaps mention one in particular on account of the specific problems of content created by the commission in itself. I refer to the complex of dwellings, industrial premises and social club that Gaudí designed and built for the Mataró Workers' Cooperative, an organization with which he had been in contact since his student days.

To my mind the principal interest of this work lies not so much in the quality of the design and the architecture as in the significance of an undertaking of this kind and in Gaudí's working on it.

Those who write on Gaudí usually emphasize his religiousness and his adherence to the ideals of order maintained by his patrons: the Güells, Milàs, Bocabellas, Batllós and other such families. In doing so they sometimes even attempt to conceal any idea of a younger Gaudí less closely connected with conservative circles and less militantly Catholic. The more dandified, agnostic Gaudí should not be ignored, even though this may have been nothing but a passing phase in the youth of a complex personality. But what helps us to explain this connection with the ideals of cooperative societies and his reading of socialist writers like Dacich, Monreau or Lavasceur, or his friendship with such notably secular characters as Ixart, Guimerà and the latter's colleague Oliveras, is the fact that in Gaudí there was a sensitivity to intellectual and human conflicts that his work endeavored to reflect at all times, and that cannot be hidden behind an image of pure sanctimoniousness. The image of Gaudí the mystic should be shown in all its force and passion. This passion was neither trivial nor purely theoretical, for it was alive to very specific problems and situations, and it represented an attempt on Gaudí's part to understand and come to terms with the contradictions revealed by the culture and society of his age.

Casa Vicens, Barcelona. Ground floor. 1883.

Design for the Güell Winery, Garraf (Barcelona).
Elevation. 1882.

ECLECTICISM AS AN EXPERIMENT

Some authors prefer to use the word "eclectic" only in speaking of Gaudí's first youthful period, when he produced the series of minor works we have been studying so far. But in my opinion the term "eclectic" should be extended, as regards Gaudí's work, to a much later date, somewhere around the turn of the century, for throughout the intervening period his work was still based to a considerable extent on references to codified historical styles. That there may have been periods of greater interest in the solutions of Moorish architecture or in those of Gothic architecture does not mean definitively that we must discount the fundamental eclecticism of the work then done by the young architect from Reus. The simultaneous or almost simultaneous references to, and use of, solutions from different historical sources are the characteristics of this architecture — the absolutely predominant note in which is, in any case, that of experiment. Gaudí's references to historical solutions are hardly ever literal in the sense of reproducing precisely measured models. On the contrary, they are nearly always reinterpretations of constructive, ornamental or functional features that are incorporated into his design without demanding any overall logic that would lead to a previously established form for the building.

In this regard I think I should add that in the work done between 1882 and 1904 it may be asserted that the overall approach to a building is frequently weaker than the effort that clearly went into the detailing and the solution of minor problems. The total conception of the buildings done during this period of eclectic experimentalism is frequently blurred by the strength of the constructional, structural or ornamental details, so that even in the more typologically convincing works, like the Palau Güell, the Teresian Convent School or Bellesguard, the parts of the building continue to overshadow the whole.

The analytical attention to such problems as architecture may create in its several aspects of light, color, space, tectonics, etc. seems to loom larger, in any event, during a period in which the historic materials are subjected to the severe test of assembly and redesigning.

Gaudí's first commissions of a certain importance came to him during the 1880s. Casa Vicens in the village of Gràcia outside Barcelona (1883–85), the holiday villa called "El Capricho" on Marquis de Comillas' estate near Comillas, Santander (1883–85), and the building intended to house the gate lodge and stables of the Güell family's estate in Les Corts, at that time on the outskirts of Barcelona (1884–87), together with the winery at Garraf, near Barcelona (1882), which were never built, form a series of parallel trials that were to reach their highest point in two works of greater architectural importance and lucidity within this group of buildings, works in which the predominant references seem to be those made to Arabic architecture. We refer to the buildings of the Palau Güell in Barcelona (1886–90) and the Teresian Convent School, also built in Barcelona (1888–90). The Casa Vicens incorporates an enormous explosion of the imagination and a brilliant display of ideas, which were to continue being developed in subsequent works. In one aspect, these were the utilization of the building styles of the Mediterranean and Arab traditions, with a mingling of materials and of tiles placed on the exterior. On the other hand, we note the marvelous and careful finish imparted to the interiors, literally Nazarí in style in one case, such as that of the ceiling of *mucarnas* in the

"El Capricho," Comillas (Santander). Ground floor. 1883.

Stables for the Güell Estate, Les Corts, Barcelona. Longitudinal section. 1884.

smoking room, while in other instances the wealth of detail of the carved and polychromed wood and the treatment of the floors and furniture give a fantastic and unreal air to the succession of spaces and outer rooms.

The gardens, the corridors enclosed by selected solutions of marquetry work, the use of variegated tiles to crown the tops of the buildings — all these give free rein to an exercise of the imagination that outdoes in its excess the iconographic sources from which it takes origin. "El Capricho" in Comillas has similar characteristics, although it is the outcome of a more limited program. Its ground plan is irregular and irresolute, without too much attention to geometry, which is always overcome by the liveliness of the textures and materials employed. A cylindrical turret, like the shaft of a column, all clad with green ceramics, is set above a pavilion formed by four monolithic columns of vaguely Romanesque inspiration. The top resembles an enormous capital, formed by radially disposed stepped corbels, on which was installed an enclosed balcony, the dome of which is supported, in a typical Gaudí caprice, by extremely light metal columns, producing the effect of a solid mass that is held up almost in nothingness.

The porter's lodge and the stables of the Güell estate in Les Corts introduce in part the treatment of an enclosing wall with a covering of false mosaic, following a free interpretation of the Spanish Mudéjar tradition. However, the area for the stables is an experiment of another kind. Vaults partitioned off in a parabolic cross section rest on arches that are a major source of light, these also parabolic, and all this structure is executed in brick. With this structure Gaudí developed a flexible system of providing an economic and versatile surfacing method, with which he had begun to experiment in the Casa Vicens, and which would continue to be characteristic of a multitude of his later buildings.

The Palau Güell in Carrer Nou de la Rambla in Barcelona was to mean the creation of a plan that was more complex, but also more unified for the purposes of a large residential building. The building rose above a ground floor, which was founded on robust cylindrical pillars; it was almost square. At all levels it surrounded a central space and it was topped by a vault, parabolic in cross-section, with tiny star-shaped openings. The various outer rooms, such as salons, vestibules, galleries and living rooms, were organized around this vertical space, with its potent feeling of centralization. The staircases and in general all the connecting spaces in this building are finished with special care, so that this results in what seems to be a deep penetration of some spaces into others, and in this way the precise delimitation of the various living rooms is broken up. Furthermore the utilization in the corridors of breaks in continuity by partitions and of double courses of columns reinforces the spatial complexity of the building as a whole. Yet it is not correct to speak of fluidity, seeing that, from the point of view of spaces, the only effects that are produced are major breaks in the closing-off of the surrounding areas and the formation of equivocal connections, which tend to complicate the possibility of transit. But for all that, the design started off with limited technical planning methods, so that even the skill in detailing tended to negate the basic planning of this architecture. The wealth of ornamentation and the variety of registers of the types of colonnades, floorings or flat ceilings that were proposed did not prevent an understanding that the basic problem that was arguable about the building was the limit imposed by its individual spatial structure.

Teresian Convent School, Barcelona.
Cross-section. 1888.

Palau Güell, Barcelona. Cross-section. 1886.

A similar problem, which presented itself less dramatically but was solved with more clarity and sobriety, was that of the Teresian Convent School, also located in Barcelona. Designed as a building of elongated rectangular form, with four floors and having a longitudinal axis for communication, this spatial theme became complicated from the moment when the circulation axis was split in two by a superimposed and subtle system of corridors formed by parabolic arcs, which, like parallel diaphragms, created an organized longitudinal form at the successive levels of the circulation space. An astute solution of the span needed for this central axis and a modified design for the openings in the upper part of the structure give this building incomparable qualities and a uniformity such as, perhaps, is not to be found in any other building by Gaudí.

From this moment on, we are able to see how the themes originating in Muslim architecture, which had so preoccupied Gaudí during this decade, slowly yielded to the reinterpretations, both personal and unrestrained, that Gaudí derived from Gothic architecture. The pinnacles of the Teresian Convent School, the series of arches on the top story, or the system of diaphragmatic arcs, characteristic of nonecclesiastical Gothic, came to dominate the final image of the building, despite the fact that walls of mixed materials, ceramics and lattice windows continue to remind us of the Mudéjar references that are the basis of many of his designs.

From the beginning of his work, Gaudí had in part surveyed the problematic aspects of the Gothic style, continually mentioning various elements or partial solutions. However, a more deliberate and global exploration of what might be called the Gothic system took place approximately during the decade of the 1890s. The two works in León — the Episcopal Palace of Astorga (1887–93) and the Casa de los Botines (1891–92) — along with the Bellesguard building in Barcelona (1900–02) and the unbuilt project for the building of the Catholic Missions in Tangier (1892–93) are the most literally Gothic experiments that Gaudí carried out during this period of his life, a period that we have designated as experimental eclecticism. Of course one must add to these works, and to this period in time, the work that he had started in 1884 for the Expiatory Church of the Sagrada Família. Gaudí went through a significant mental process when engaged on this unfinished work, which was a summary of all his architectural vicissitudes, since the project for this "Grand Temple" went through phases and varying periods, according to the way in which Gaudí's architectural personality matured and took form; thus, during a first stage it was very much academically Gothic, closely following the initial Gothic Revival project of the pioneer of the church, Francisco de Paula del Villar, but it was to follow more personal and free interpretations of that expressive building system, which permitted a profound reflection on the scope and possibilities of the Gothic system, which would be so decisive for Gaudí's subsequent work. Thus the initial elaboration of the Sagrada Família and of the nonecclesiastic Gothic buildings, mentioned above, may be considered to be the stage of his most explicit critical thought about the possibilities of utilizing the architecture of a specific period of history, just as in previous years he had come close to Arab and Mudéjar architecture.

Although its roof was not completed according to Gaudí's plan, the Episcopal Palace of Astorga stressed the theme of a central space, which was to organize the vertical circulation and the surrounding principal rooms in the form of a square plan, topped at the corners by cylindrical

Project for the Catholic Missions in Tangier.
Elevation. 1892.

Episcopal Palace, Astorga (León). Cross-section. 1887.

"Casa de los Botines," León. Main elevation. 1891.

towers, and by others that rose above the wings for the throne room, the chapel, the library and the reception salon. Despite the fact that few examples of it were built, this floor scheme was one of those most customarily put forward by Gaudí throughout his life, and in which there is most noted the aftereffects of the would-be academic philosophy of history as taught at that time in the schools of Europe. The symmetry in design, the standardized character of the multiple solutions for windows, colonnades, capitals, balustrades, buttresses, etc., a certain coarseness in the arrangement of the masonry made from white granite from Bierzo — these brought about a solution that was feeble enough for this castle, so closely allied to the copies of a new ground plan brought into fashion by the followers of Viollet-le-Duc.

The Fernández Andrés house, more popularly called "Casa de los Botines" in central León, has similar characteristics, although perhaps the need for this building to accommodate everyday living obliged the architect to cut down on the treatment of the global mass of the structure, by means of a more customary and repetitive system of openings, superimposed floors and roofs.

Yet if these two buildings can in some manner be understood as an exercise of trial and error with the language of the Gothic, the rebuilding of a country house on a site where there had existed a small and ancient villa, built by King Martin the Humane in the foothills of Tibidabo with views over the plain of Barcelona, may be seen as much more ambitious in scope. Bellesguard is a building of approximately square design, flanked by a lofty tower with an enclosed viewing balcony, and topped by the characteristic four-armed crucifix that Gaudí so often put in place as the culminating point of his buildings. The Gothic touches in the façades, though allusive, are not literal but have a metaphoric nature, which is the result of a redesign in which neither the form of the material, nor its lightness, nor the proportions produce anything more than a parody of the historical forms reintroduced in the building.

As regards the interiors, these he executed with still more freedom. Certainly there are Gothic themes, but these may at best be referred to as being in parentheses. His preoccupation with structure, as is evident in the attic, the main rooms, or in the semibasement, or the resolution of the staircase, shows that he was continuing to think about the structural problem involving free-standing colonnades, which he had extracted from the interpretation of the Gothic spirit put forward by Viollet-le-Duc. What happened was that this line of thought was continually becoming more personal, free and creative, and furthermore it did not constitute a mere eclectic imitation, but was an innovative experiment based on proposals derived from a definite historic architecture.

In this account of several periods of the history of architecture, it is necessary to single out the stimuli of invention and of planned solutions of an original nature, which were peculiar to the architecture of his era. Thus, in our opinion, as regards the thinking of Gaudí around the beginning of this century, it is necessary to consider and to add to the account the apartment house that Gaudí was to build for Pere Màrtir Calvet on Carrer de Casp in Barcelona (1898–1904). The project originated in the usual type of organization of neighborhood housing blocks in the Eixample of that time, which followed in the tracks of a well-established architectural idea of the period. This consisted of two apartment units on each floor, surrounding four open spaces for interior ventilation, with a double façade facing the street and the inner courtyard of the block.

Stylistically, this building corresponds, in terms of ornamentation, to the various baroque ideas that can be seen reinterpreted in the balconies and bay windows of the main façade, the use of helicoidal columns in the vestibule and the well of the main staircase, and the supple top of the façade with a double curvilinear gable end, which is certainly inspired by the Baroque.

We must note here that basically the rear façade of the building is perhaps the most creative part, with no stylistic references from elsewhere; here Gaudí reinterpreted the customary solution of rear galleries using the more complex finish of a continuous line of small and large balconies so as to blend the light and make use of the spaces between the balconies. Actually this contribution began to constitute more than an ornamental re-creation of historical styles and it presented problems of reexamination of a type which not long afterward would become more radical in Casa Batlló (1904–06) and Casa Milà (1906–10). But we have already pointed out that this first period in Gaudí of confrontation with historical styles is in fact an analytical and experimental era, but it was not as yet common for him to arrive at synthetic formulations; on the other hand the period was dominated by the drive to understand, prolong and go beyond an eclectic reception of historic tradition.

Several conclusions make it possible to describe the character of this first period of Gaudí's creations, all of them being in fact associated with a reinterpretation of style.

In the first place there is the breaking up of the global composition so as to enhance the fragments. It is important to indicate how, during this first era, despite its proximity to Gaudí's scholastic apprenticeship, his work is formed in overall composition in a manner very different from the rules of academic composition. To be exact, Gaudí's ground plans, elevations and cross-sections, which for some reason are not abundant as documents, do not have the capacity to *explain* their art, as in academic architecture. It is the attention paid to the problems of individual parts, the splitting up of the edifice into a multitude of individual pieces, that characterizes this first period. A rupture with the custom of dividing space into boxes, appropriate for an architecture of the masses, is also a first consequence of the same attitude toward space. Gaudí still had not formulated a plastic form for fluidity and continuity, but he had established the basis for this by means of alterations in the orthogonal wall construction, usual at that time for building problems such as he had to resolve. Breaking up the enclosed areas formed by the compartmentalization by walls was the result of the attention he paid, piece by piece, to structural problems, illumination and the textures of the finishes.

Furthermore, this stage of experimenting by Gaudí established a technique typical of modern thinking, that of a distancing from what had gone before. We have seen that Gaudí's architecture in this period was made up of constant allusions to historic architecture, with re-creations of themes already codified and metaphors of forms long known. But this linguistic technique,

Torre Bellesguard, Barcelona. Cross-section. 1900.

Casa Calvet, Barcelona. Standard
floor plan. 1898.

Casa Calvet.

which originates in an eclectic conception, according to which the character of the building can be created only by means of mechanisms of relationship, through which we refer back to established linguistic codes (such as may be the case for well-defined systems of style in archaeology and historiography), was used by Gaudí as a more subtle manipulation. He did not quote from it literally. He did not imitate it obediently. On the contrary, there was a more perverse process of distancing, by which changes in scale, format, construction solutions of arrangement and detailing do not refer directly to established sources, but there is interposed a barrier of novelty and change, which makes his language a constant stimulus to create the unexpected. Of course it was this aspect that subsequently fascinated the Surrealists when they came in contact with the work of Gaudí.

This distancing of meaning is related to another linguistic technique, typical of Gaudí's architecture, which appeared from the beginning and which is the third characteristic we wish to point out. This aspect is the freedom of association of ideas which the architect made part of his work. We have already referred to the lack of guidelines, which may be seen in his buildings from the moment of first planning. The particular point of academic architecture is that from the very beginning the order of events is to be left unchanged without surprises, so that the development of the building is to proceed along fixed lines. Now, on the contrary, this did not exist for Gaudí, who at no time whatever produced buildings in a style that had been guided by principles of coherence. Neither the form of the complex, nor references dominated by a certain style, nor the method of building eliminate the possibility of being surprised by brusque changes of theme, by the association of themes that seem separate, or by a simple collage of iconographic materials emanating from various sources. In this aspect of Gaudí there is something that connects him with the most marked features of the Anglo-Saxon picturesque tradition, which is as much as to say, with one of the fundamental sources, perhaps the most fundamental, of modern sensibility. The creation of an aesthetic effect as a result of the free association of feelings was translated into architecture by a process of design in which nothing is determined beforehand and in which the means used may possibly involve surprise and psychological shock.

Finally, as a further observation of the characteristics evident in this era of Gaudí's experimental eclecticism, and which were to continue in later works, it is necessary to point out that the search for the essential in every problem stands out as a method of work characteristic of that architect.

Solutions to the design conflicts that appear in any given work can be resolved by harmonizing them with other problems, with other exigencies that are involved in the development of the building. But there is another possibility, which is that in reacting to a conflict that appears as critical, and that may well be essential, all the stress may be laid on what is considered as happening by chance, and that may be relegated as not existing. In this period, this form of radicalism appeared in Gaudí in the design of furniture — that of the Palau Güell or of Casa Calvet — to the point where emphasis on the structure of a basement, a staircase or a roof, or the redesign of a window or a turret comes into conflict with the notion of coherence or of equilibrium, which has always been propounded by the classical tradition.

THE SYNTHESIS OF *MODERNISME*

In the work of Gaudí, the first decade of the 20th century was to coincide with a time of synthesis, which, although fragile, represented the culminating point of his work, and above all, of all his efforts to produce a new architecture.

Many critics have accepted with what is perhaps excessive benevolence this idea of producing a new architecture as put forward by Gaudí and many other architects of the time. Certainly during the last years of eclectic culture, the general clamor in Europe and America for a new style, for a language differing from those of historical origin, for an expression of the yearnings and changes of modern civilization, was almost constantly in evidence. Gaudí also participated in this universal desire, and in quite a few ways he was motivated by it. His disciples and followers certainly thought that Gaudí had achieved this, since his work constituted a fundamental contribution to this new art — Art Nouveau — of modern times.

The years which we are about to analyze are precisely those in which these hopes were cherished, and possibly they were the years during which was concocted the interpretation of a *Modernista* Gaudí, that is to say, of an architect who was contributing in a clear and positive way to modern building and self-expression. It is well known that the term *Modernisme* meant in Catalonia what in other European cities was to be called Art Nouveau, Jugendstil, Sezession, Liberty, Floreale, etc. Gaudí's position within this cultural and aesthetic current, called *Modernisme* in Catalonia, is at most tangential. We cannot deny that he formed part of this broad movement, but it is no less certain that he consciously placed himself as one who was critical and reacting, as regards the progressive lay aestheticism to be found as the basic ideology of the most distinguished *Modernistes*.

In any case, however, once we have taken into account this peculiar affinity in some aspects, but rejection in others, in relation to the phenomenon of *Modernisme*, it must be said that if at any given time the affinities prevailed over the discrepancies, it was precisely during the years at the beginning of the 20th century, perhaps when *Modernisme* in literature and painting had begun to decline.

These were the years when there was a decisive change in public estimation of the figure and the work of Gaudí. Hitherto his work had been little appreciated and even rejected as being incomprehensible and extravagant. In Barcelona even avant-garde circles and magazines seemed to pay little attention to him. This appreciation changed at the beginning of the century. Gaudí began to be interpreted by his disciples and critics as a genius; as if he were a genuine contribution that Catalan art and culture were making to world culture, and as having for this reason a value, not just respectable, but also worthy of praise and enthusiasm beyond the limits of questioning. With the development of Catalan politics, personages indigenous to local culture became the objects of special veneration. This was, *inter alia,* the case with Gaudí. He passed from rejection to praise, from incomprehension to being valued for his work, which was seen as being an essential contribution to contemporary artistic and architectural culture. Nowadays, almost a century later, our evaluation is less enthusiastic in terms of these ready reckoners of modernity and of the future, although perhaps it might be greater taking into account his originality and above all the intensity of the passion distilled by his works. If we do not believe overmuch in the modernity of Gaudí and in his character as a precursor of the architecture of the 20th century, the thing that impresses us above all nowadays is the tremendous force and dramatic power innate in him, which were able to assimilate the contradictions of the architecture of his time.

After all, it is certain that during the years that we are about to analyze, and despite a few of his works that were important and completed, Gaudí managed to condense a certain synthesis of the different problems that were on the point of discovery. This was a synthesis, which although it was unstable, fluid, changeable, managed to express a maturity and a sureness of touch that we do not find in previous eras. Although his own capacity as a critic was to lead him to make new reexaminations, it is certain that it was in these years that the originality of his language and its consonance with other parallel European experiments was made manifest in its clearest form.

Eusebi Güell's interest in the ideas of English social reformers was to influence his development of two initiatives, one the construction of a residential suburb in the style of a garden city, Park Güell (1900–14), and the other an industrial settlement in Santa Coloma de Cervelló (1890–1915). Güell regarded himself, along with other intellectuals, architects and politicians of the beginning of the century, as being one of the defenders of the ideas of Ebenezer Howard, and the result of this interest in the new way of understanding the growth of industrial cities as part of a new hegemony was the creation of the Social Museum (1909) and of the Civic Society for the Garden City (1912).

The plan for Park Güell as carried out by Gaudí consisted of the organization of a residential area for single-family living units, isolated in a country estate on the Muntanya Pelada in the Tres Turons district of Barcelona. A total of 60 blocks of land, triangular in form and spread over the steep side of the mountain, were to make up the offer of land for building residences of good quality in a sunny area, with splendid views over the city and the sea in the distance. Gaudí's work consisted of sketches of the street plan, the limits of the estate and the building plan of services necessary for the proper functioning of this isolated residential nucleus.

The only buildings in the true sense of the word were the two on each side of the main entry to the park, which were to house the porter's lodge and the administration. For these purposes Gaudí designed two blocks of approximately circular ground plan, with their proportions made deliberately vertical, with roofs formed by curved surfaces, executed in vaults of brick sealed by rapid-acting mortar, according to the traditional Catalan method. The administration block had in addition a pointed steeple, the most notable characteristic of which was that it was the first trial by Gaudí of the use of reinforced concrete incorporating steel rods. This entire fantasy of roofs, like the coping of the top of the wall surrounding these buildings, in the middle of which one finds the entry gate, is covered with portions of broken ceramic (trencadís) which, set out over the complex geometrical surfaces of these volumes, give the buildings a showy and surprising look.

General layout of Park Güell on the slopes of the Muntanya Pelada, Barcelona. Plan. 1900.

Gaudí went on to build accesses and outside staircases in the manner of an imaginative cascade and fountain, presided over by a mythological figure of a lizard. But perhaps the most interesting component is the hypostyle hall meant to be a local market for the use of the inhabitants of the park, and also the large lookout plaza, which formed the roof of the market. The hypostyle hall consisted of a free interpretation of the classical theme of the telesterion, but with a completely subjective version of the classical column and the molding of the friezes. In fact, the spaces between the columns were covered over by domes partitioned off in the form of a spherical cap, which served as supports for the plaza above and as a conduit for the water drained off from it, which was then deposited in a large cistern below the market, for use in the Park Güell itself.

The most outstanding element of the plaza, apart from the spatial power of this large flat surface, which contrasted with the irregular slope of the mountain, was the balustrade and bench in combination, which set the limits of the plaza above the colonnade. Originating quite empirically from the ergonomic profile of a human in a sitting position, to establish the type of cross-section, this bench follows a serpentine course along the edge of the plaza forming meanders, corners and lesser spaces, intended as meeting places for strollers and other users of this public area.

Together with its form, what turned out to be the most original part was the lavishness of its coloring, achieved, as were most of the design elements of the park, by covering its sinuous and capricious surfaces with broken glazed ceramics, forming a spectacular collage of fragments.

Finally we should observe the entire system of elevated viaducts, some sloping, that formed the network of communications in Park Güell, and that were to provide access to the plots of land. Stout inclined pillars, the bodies of which were continuous between arch, capital and base, and clad in stone hewn from the sites where they were placed, were built to form elegant arcades, above which ran the roadways. The precision of the calculation of the thrusts involved links up with the plastic fluidity innate in this complex, whose static outline, strength of form and ornamental finish combine in a unique and dynamic result. It is in Park Güell that references to historical styles are abandoned by Gaudí, who now makes use of a language of which the continuity of the surfaces, the use of complex geometrical forms and the splendor of the color and the finishes constitute the most specific aspect of the contribution of Gaudí to the *Modernista* blossoming of the turn of the century.

The rebuilding of Casa Batlló, which Gaudí undertook during this same period (1904–06), must be thought of in the same way. Its clear aim was to soften the rigidity of style that had become standard for the type of house found in the Eixample of Barcelona. For this purpose, Gaudí modified the inner courtyard of the dwelling, giving it dynamism through the incorporation of a staircase with a tautly undulating outline, introducing an ascending linear motif that combined perfectly with the treatment of light in this vertical space. In effect, by means of a gradation in shade of the blue of the ceramic facing of this central courtyard, and a redesign of the windows

Casa Batlló, Barcelona. Longitudinal section. 1904.

that opened on to it, the sequence of vestibule–staircase–first floor–central courtyard was transformed into an ever-changing space, in which lines, color and light all contribute to an atmosphere of fantasy and wonder.

As regards the remodeling of the façade, Gaudí redesigned the openings, especially those of the ground and first floors, by means of enormous apertures formed by a support structure of stone, which left free (but as part of the structure) small window holes in a vaguely symmetrical arrangement. Above these forms, the remainder of the façade, undulating and faced with colored tiles and pieces of glass, provided one of the most subtle polychrome decorations of the era of *Modernisme*, all this being topped by a tower in the form of a floral bulb, with a tiled roof reminiscent of the spiny backbone of some mythological animal.

The enigmatic form of the balconies, the stained-glass windows of the openings, the finish of the floors and ceilings and the furnishings that Gaudí designed for this house all show how the architect commanded in his maturity a breadth of register that was perfectly capable of solving the problems that he himself had posed, by so freely rethinking the forms established by the architecture of the time. An intense yet abstract naturalism, evocative of floral, animal and geological motifs, and a capacity for exploiting these themes on a contrasting and variable scale, as well as providing in profusion a mode of creating a feeling of fragile instability, offer in Casa Batlló a clear example of the degree of brilliance and sureness of touch possessed by Gaudí's work at this mature stage.

Yet perhaps the most ambitious metropolitan building, and the one that best demonstrates the Gaudí style — if we may call it such — during these years, was the house that from 1906 on was built for Roser Milà in the center of Barcelona, on the corner of Passeig de Gràcia and Carrer de Provença.

Gaudí designed this building as a complex of spacious apartments, which were distributed from the corner façade and around courtyards of approximately circular shape, on both sides of the angular ground plan of the site. It seems that there was an initial idea of giving most of these courtyards a dimension such as would permit the construction of a helicoidal ramp, up which vehicles could ascend to service the different floors and apartments. Whether or not this was a lasting idea, the fact is that a design planning a structure around large courtyards was a fundamental modification of construction on corners, which until then had been tried out as a solution proposed by Barcelona architects for the construction of corner buildings with beveled angles, such as were typified by the designs of Cerdà for the Eixample.

At this level of choice of type, as well as at levels of construction and ornament, it is clear that during these years Gaudí clear-sightedly rejected all the established solutions in an audacious exploration of different types of architectural structure.

The planimetric solution for Casa Milà, popularly called "La Pedrera" (Stone Quarry), is a good example of this. The experiment is innovative even in its method of building. To the traditional

Casa Milà ("La Pedrera"), Barcelona.
Ground floor. 1906.

rectilinear structure of load-bearing walls, forming systems of parallel corridors, Gaudí opposed
a system of a free ground plan formed by a metal structure of pillars and trusses of girders.
The structural solution of "La Pedrera" is complex because of the irregularity of its correlations, and
because of the differences in load brought about by the interior courtyards, the façade and the
support needed for the basement, so that it can be used as a garage. In any case, the ways in which
floors are divided into apartments are of such diversity and mobility as to have nothing in common
with the rectilinear geometry that was traditional for the interior spaces of an apartment building.
The clash of uneven and undulating planes, which form convex courses and spatial obstructions,
is reinforced by a careful ornamentation of the ceilings and the floorings, executed with a skill and
an imagination that are quite unique. As for the handling of the façade, it must be said that this is
one of the most potent and perverse of all Gaudí's works. To propose the stone of Vilafranca, with
its massiveness and density, coarsely smoothed down so that it involved inevitable projections of the
surface, and to express in such a medium all this fluidity and dynamism, like the to and fro of a kind
of surging wave, was undoubtedly an idea as potent as it was contradictory. It is certain that in
this very contradiction one finds the attraction of his audacity; and further, the surprise and upset
that is imposed on us by this façade is due to the fact that he has managed to master and mold
a material that is physically and visually heavy with the aim of expressing precisely the opposite:
lightness and ceaseless undulation. In any case, this precocious Surrealism, which was to make
such an appeal to the Surrealists years later, demonstrates, in this mannered technique of the
contradictory use of forms and materials, a consummate example.

Finally we should point out that the roof too is original and unusual. Formed by a system coursing
along the length of the façade of diaphragmatic and parabolic arcs in brick, the resulting volume
consists of a sort of attic, in which the internal space gives the impression of an inverted ship's
framework, or the internal structure of some nameless animal of gigantic dimensions. It is
precisely this fantastic suggestion of gigantic size or of something in a dream that is seen
once more in the solution of large chimneys which, like enormous sculptures, all different,
form a top to the flat roof of Casa Milà. Developing the experiment of complex geometrical
surfaces that started in the pavilions of Park Güell, and utilizing in the same way a ceramic
cladding of *trencadís* (ceramic fragments), the flat roof and the chimneys of "La Pedrera"
represent in their lightness and fantasy a brilliant counterpoint to the darkness and dramatic
quality of the stone façade.

We would also like to comment on another work of this period, which we have called the synthesis
of *Modernisme*. We refer to the work of restoration and readaptation of the choir and chancel of
the cathedral of Palma de Mallorca, which Gaudí with his assistants and collaborators undertook
between 1904 and 1914. The work consisted mostly of removing the choir, which was located in
the center of the main nave, so as to install it near the chancel, bringing it forward by one section
of the nave, closer to the pulpit. In this way there was a transformation of the pulpit, the site
and illumination of the main altar, the stained-glass windows and some lateral altars, with some
additional minor work. The work in Mallorca was not major from the viewpoint of the volume of
work actually accomplished, but it showed a new sensitivity in the perception of a historic structure,
such as the great Gothic fabric of the cathedral, and also a capacity to alter these venerable stone

structures, without any undesirable carry-over from philosophies of history or ideas of archaeological reconstruction.

The work involved re-creating the clarity permitted by the perfection of the Gothic structure of this cathedral, so much admired by Gaudí and his collaborators, by both eliminating the choir and creating, by the use of lamps, a mobile suspended canopy and the new setting for the chancel, an ambience that had nothing in common with the traditional Gothic atmosphere, nor even with the later transformations that this had undergone.

In the work in the cathedral of Palma de Mallorca the presence of collaborators was of no small importance. Joan Rubió and Josep Maria Jujol as architects, Josep Llimona and Joan Rebull as sculptors, not to mention stained-glass makers, locksmiths and other artisans, contributed to the final result in a decisive way.

On this point we must note here a controversial issue, on which it is difficult to come to definite conclusions. This is the matter of the relationship between Gaudí and his collaborators, and the extent of the contribution of the latter to the splendor and completeness of the architect's work. Certainly the technical ability of Rubió and the conscientious aid given by Berenguer are well recognized in some of the works. Yet the most disputed contribution, precisely because of the importance that one can sense it had, was that of the architect Josep Maria Jujol. The period that we are discussing, that of the most complete *Modernisme* of Gaudí, coincided with the years of direct collaboration with Jujol, first as a student and then as a young qualified architect in Gaudí's studio. It is known that Jujol played a personal part in certain definite works, such as the bench surrounding the plaza of the Park Güell, the ironwork of the balconies of the Casa Milà and the ornamentation of the new choir in the cathedral of Palma de Mallorca.

It is certain that later on, when Jujol went on working on his own account, these qualities and personal features continued, and they show his enormous capacity for plastic and color creation, as well as his long-standing taste for organic undulating forms, which are always evoked by a working method that is taut and alive.

We are not trying to affirm that this period of the synthesis of *Modernisme* in Gaudí was in reality the work of Jujol, for that would be an enormous exaggeration. Yet what we do think certain is that the culmination of skill and driving energy seen in the work of Gaudí during those years cannot be evaluated without recognizing the major contribution that in the matter of ornamental finishes must be attributed to the ability and taste of his young assistant.

Our interpretation is that for Gaudí there was a cycle, which passed from experimental eclecticism in his early years to an architecture of destruction in his last works, with an intermediate period of equilibrium and synthesis, which we have denoted as being the most specifically *Modernista*. Thus the point we wish to make very clear is that in our opinion, despite all the transformation and inversion, his architecture at that time was an exceptional synthesis of the assimilation of historical styles and the consummation of all his new departures toward the future and the end of his adventure in architecture.

TOWARD DESTRUCTION

From 1908 on, Gaudí concentrated on very few works, which apart from the Sagrada Família, which was to occupy the rest of his days, denote a certain radical change in attitudes that were already to be found in his earlier projects.

It is worth noting that in this final period of his life the architect did not re-create his own successes, not even the certainty and confidence of the *Modernista* synthesis, achieved in the years immediately preceding. On the contrary, it could be said that his work at this time was trying to pursue still further the possibilities of his discoveries through works that ultimately proved impossible but that, by his inability to complete them, were to become a symbol of the titanic force of the architecture of Gaudí.

It was precisely during these years that his work began to receive recognition beyond the local frontiers, so that both a commission for an early plan for a Grand Hotel in New York (1908), and the exhibition of his work in the Société Nationale de Beaux Arts in Paris in 1910, indicated the contradiction of a success in distant places, while the young Noucentistes (Men of the 1900s) in Barcelona began to distance themselves from the uncontrolled euphoria of the master from Reus.

The two most important works that these years brought forth were the hotel already mentioned, which never came to fruition, and the beginning of the building of the church of Colònia Güell, a project to which Gaudí devoted years of reflection and work, and the foundation stone for which was laid in 1908.

The characteristics of both these commissions displayed, in one way, a clear polarity. On one side, there was the grandiose American hotel, which could have taken Gaudí to the highest places in the international talent market. This would have been a triumph for the most attractive and post-eclectic aspect of Gaudí, as this existed at the beginning of the century, and it would have embodied all the decorative and symbolic display with which he approached it. Work on the church did finally begin, although the construction was dramatically halted in 1915; its dimensions were of the usual kind and the needs of organic form and coherency were observed with an almost biological conception of its structure.

The idea of a demonstration of large dimensions and a great display of decor seem to have been the attractions of an impossible voyage to America, which never came about, and which, if it had, would have substantially modified the final stages of Gaudí's life.

On the contrary, his work was limited to two churches, so that he devoted himself in the last years of his life almost totally to them. We shall leave to the end of this work an analysis of the Sagrada

Project for a hotel in New York City. Cross-section. 1908.

Família, which in itself as a building is almost a summary of Gaudí's biography. Nevertheless, we shall in this section analyze the other church by Gaudí, although it was not completed either; in it, the violence of his planning approach and the radical way it was set out led Gaudí to what was actually a language of architectural destruction, in which the parts and the whole do not appear to be a reasoned process of composition, but on the contrary, the elements seem to be dispersed members, fragments only half planed into shape, which, with indomitable force, the architect tried to put together in opposition to a destructive hurricane that was leading to dislocation and a whirlwind of chaos.

Around 1908 there appeared to be a true contradiction in these two buildings: this was between the universal and metropolitan Gaudí who could have come into being, and the solipsistic and elusive Gaudí, who was not to be fully realized either.

When, in 1908, a New York multimillionaire chanced to visit Barcelona, he was greatly impressed when he went to see Park Güell and Casa Milà, both recently finished. Since he was a good businessman, he translated his surprise at Gaudí's work into a concrete proposal; it was a matter of studying the possibilities of building a great hotel in the city of skyscrapers, which would challenge, in its building method and its decorative and symbolic splendor, the modern buildings then being erected in the great American metropolis. Gaudí's plan was like a great secular cathedral, and it made use, although turning them in another direction, of ideas that were already in preparation for his plans for churches.

The building, some three hundred meters in height, similar to the Eiffel Tower in Paris, or to the future Chrysler Building in New York, was to have had a circular ground plan, in the form of a monumental spindle, surrounded by similar forms on all sides. The result was a clustering and ascending complex, crowned with a powerful beacon in the shape of a star, full of symbolism and fantasy. The composition of the building carried to a further extent ideas that had appeared in Casa Milà. The central nucleus of the great tower had superimposed on it a hall and six enormous dining rooms in various styles; five of them were in the indigenous styles of different parts of the world, and the sixth was to change according to the festivities to be held in it. A circular nave with parabolic arcades on two successive floors formed its upper part, above a large auditorium for several thousand spectators.

Gaudí seemed to adapt to American megalomania in this project, which never got beyond a simple sketch, since the further development of his ideas never came to completion. In any case it is worth noting that he showed a capacity, both in the discussions and the experiments that he had at that time planned, to respond to propositions as ostentatiously modern as this. Probably neither the technology nor the imagery fitted in with American aspirations of the time. It is certain that in this, his last attempt to plan in terms of an advanced industrial society, Gaudí's project, for all its grandeur, was a lost opportunity, a definite chance that would have profoundly changed his orientation and importance. With the vanishing of this impossible American dream, Gaudí remained confronted with his usual problems in a society that was traditional and protobourgeois, under the double spell of a decaying historical architecture and a new architecture, which could no

Crypt of the church of Colònia Güell, Santa Coloma de Cervelló (Barcelona).
Floor plan of the structure. c. 1908.

Photograph of the inverted scale model for the structure of
the church of Colonia Güell. c. 1900.

longer be expected to develop either from experimentalism in building or from the naturalistic
expressionism of its propositions.

The church for Colònia Güell, on the other hand, was the monumental culmination of a vast
operation undertaken by Eusebi Güell to endow his textile industry not only with a healthy and
peaceful workforce, with harmony between employers and workers and between manufacturing
production and a natural way of life, but also presided over, as in an ancient classical city, by a
temple situated on a small acropolis, close at hand, yet sufficiently distant, to watch over and keep
in order the coherence of the complex.

According to Josep Ràfols, it seems that Gaudí had been working on the plans of this church since
1898, even though the construction did not begin until ten years later.

The first designs for this building were in structural coherence, leading the way to a complete definition
of the form of the church. A critical survey of the Christian church, and in particular of the Gothic
cathedral, were not to be carried out in parts, in a fragmentary fashion, using a redesign of arches
and vaults, but had to lead to a total definition of the structure, with a three-dimensional system
of the distribution of stresses. The method of reversed tensions that Gaudí used to define the form
of the church in Colònia Güell is actually an experimental method that tried to make use of a well-
interconnected system, which at any moment, and in all its parts, would respond to modifications in
weights or measures that might occur at any given point. This made the problem of the structure
supporting the building seem an absolute priority. His construction of tension cables, with bags full of
buckshot proportional to the loads at any given point, and sited so as to provide tension rather than
equilibrium, was an ingenious empirical procedure for approximately measuring the distribution of
forces in a static structure where everything produced compression. By this means Gaudí, who was
putting forward the idea that it was possible to have a meticulous understanding of a complete
structure, in which supporting and supported elements would be synonymous, limited himself to
a method of working with materials that was quite usual in the tradition of building with stone;
this led, inevitably, to a complete self-limitation in his experiments, and undoubtedly in a far from
innovative direction.

We are familiar from photographs with his experiments with this maquette of inverted cablework;
there are also photographs taken from various viewpoints with the aim of making available views
of the future building and its outlines. Everything in this plan exudes organicism, despite the initial
technical aspects of the planning. Notions of continuity and homogeneity of structure seem to
comprise the essence of an idea that in actual construction would be handled with profound
radicalism and austerity of expression.

In contrast, the ground plan of the church, as far as we know, was Gaudí's most fully completed
effort to resolve in the form of a centralized design the main body of the building of a church.
The idea of centralism in Gaudí's spaces was a theme that grew more insistent as his architecture
matured. However, the center that his forms of architecture needed to specify was not, according
to academic tradition, a geometric site defined by abstract symmetry. On the contrary, his utilization

Crypt of the church of Colònia Güell, Santa Coloma de Cervelló (Barcelona). Longitudinal section. c. 1908.

of space is the result of an effort to aim programs and structures in the direction of that cosmic and stable order that a center has represented in almost all cultures. For Gaudí, the church had to be the site of centralism and of hierarchy. Centralism is certainly an idea that is constant throughout the long European classical tradition; it was revived at the dawn of the 20th century, when the intricate spaces of the arts of the Sezession, the transparencies of metal structures or the explosion outward seen in the spaces proposed by Frank Lloyd Wright, were abolishing this archetype of composition. The hierarchy still implies the survival of the classical notion of space composed of reciprocally dependent structures; for these structures there is always a clear stratification of spatial values, according to which they are incorporated into a single mononuclear system.

It is worth noting that in the case of the church of Colònia Güell, these forms of hierarchy and centralism are not achieved by the simple application of a previously established geometrical or typological model, but by a titanic and involved effort at shaping anew these superimpositions; however, this is done by means of a polyvalent flow of incidental reciprocal influences and organic inter-relationships, which the building seems to suggest by its analogy with a living organism. Yet in the church of Colónia Güell, what contrasts with these desires for organic unification of space by means of structural modeling is the design of the elements that are integrated into the actual building process.

In this phase of Gaudí's work there is a decided return to the elemental and the primitive. This primitivist movement should not surprise us, since it coincides culturally with what was being carried out by contemporary artists in other fields of art; this answered the need to find, in the primitive, roots that had existed previously in the historical diversification of styles. If, in one of Gaudí's first periods, we can identify an obvious eclecticism that had recourse to diverse sources in search of inspiration for his new architecture, and later on, a fluid synthesis in which stylistic molds seem to disintegrate into a doughy material, capable of being shaped into endless continuities, now toward the end of his life, Gaudí in this creation of the church of Colónia Güell seems to return to the crudeness of gestures, to a rough sketch of basic forms and the elemental nature of the resources involved. The crypt built for Colónia Güell is a brutal display of this elemental and primitive vocabulary. The columns have been reduced to the juxtaposition of three stones, crudely hewn, which imitate base, shaft and capital schematically. The arches and domes demonstrate crudely the placing of their elements of construction, brick and stone, in a brutal exhibition of their normally hidden constructive elements. Lintels, doors and windows with capricious but basic forms are in reality explaining a construction that in its radical simplification is trying to take us back to monolithism and to the rudimentary actions of the task of building.

There is in the crypt of Colónia Güell, as in no other building by Gaudí, a sharp contrast of audacity and the interconnection of the structures, and the spatial result, which is fluid, mobile and fleeting, and furthermore one that is achieved with a limited and abstract repertoire of building elements.

Thus the extreme severity and sophistication in the concept of the body of building represented by this edifice are finally expressed through a voluntary and ascetic primitivism, which moves from harshness to violence.

The effort of synthesis put into this church, as an important structure and as a system of space, is resolved by an abstract dismemberment of the architectural components, which, with its crushed appearance of stonework joined by chance, manages to produce the paradox of a destructive construction.

THE CHURCH OF THE SAGRADA FAMÍLIA: A SUMMARY AND DISCUSSION OF THE WORK OF GAUDÍ

We have already pointed out that confidence in industrial progress and in the social changes produced by this new life was not shared by all sectors of opinion. In some conservative circles, the transformations being brought about, although they were leading at the same time to certain positive achievements, were also considered to be the cause of moral disorder, loss of traditional values and a social crisis.

Within this current of criticism, one must take into account the leadership of Josep Maria Bocabella, founder of the Spiritual Association of Devotees of St. Joseph, which in 1881 had managed to accumulate sufficient funds to acquire an enormous building site, which occupied all of one block of Cerdà's Eixample on the plain of Barcelona. They wanted to erect there a church dedicated to the exaltation of the figures of St. Joseph and of the Holy Family, as symbols of the stability and ordered family life that were deemed to be basic pillars of the social order.

The proposal of this association was an ambitious one, inasmuch as it involved not only the construction of a large church in a new expansion area of the city, but also, in the minds of the promoters, this church was to be accompanied by schools, halls for meetings and workshops that would allow the creation of a true social center for the new metropolis. From the viewpoint of the Catholic religion, the exaltation of the figure of St. Joseph had grown throughout the 19th century, especially when he was seen as the patron of the movements that the Catholic Church was sponsoring as a reply to the growing lay and anticlerical movements of workers. A clear traditionalism, combined with the exaltation of the family and of craftwork, were the best-defined characteristics of this ideological attitude.

However, this project of a church, which initially came into being with the idea of a site of commemoration, around which it was imagined that a social center could be created, grew rapidly in the scope of its ambition when it was given the opportunity of becoming the cathedral of the new city. A neomedievalist idea took form and pervaded the minds of all of the group of personalities who were promoting this church. In the same way in which the integrated medieval society was centered around a great building, which dominated the labors of the citizens, so also the new metropolis, which was growing almost limitlessly, should have its new center in a great architectural monument, around which would be centered, in a visual and symbolic manner, the new society that would become established in its surroundings. At first it was called the Cathedral of the Poor, taking its name from the vein of compassion for poverty that ran through society at the turn of the century, but afterward it was called the New Cathedral, openly accepting the idea

Church of the Sagrada Família, Barcelona. Floor plan. c. 1906.

that it was the whole of the new city that was to be endowed with a new center and spiritual guide. The project of the Church of the Sagrada Família (Holy Family) was to go on increasing in its ambition, not only from the architectural point of view, but also as a representative and social creation.

The commission was given originally to the architect of the diocese, Francisco de Paula del Villar, and the foundation stone of the new church was laid on St. Joseph's Day, 1882. Del Villar's plan was academically Gothic Revival and of much smaller dimensions than it was eventually to have in the hands of Gaudí. Not long after work began, when the excavation and formation of the foundations of the crypt were proceeding, disagreements occurred between the association and the architect, and these brought work to a halt and it was proposed that del Villar should be replaced by another architect. Rather oddly, the new commission ended up with the young Gaudí, probably thanks to the mediation of Joan Martorell, the architect of the association, a prestigious figure and one well acquainted with both the dismissed architect and the future candidate, although he may have been influenced by the fact that Gaudí had for some time been a collaborator in del Villar's studio.

In 1883, Gaudí at the age of thirty-one took charge of the work and began a revision in depth of the project, which was to go on throughout his life. The first objective was to increase the dimensions of the building, taking as his guide the idea of a new cathedral. Seemingly Gaudí also studied a change of location, since the site on which the edifice had been started did not allow either a maximum use of the building plot or a more unusual and monumental arrangement of the church.

The town planning position of which Gaudí was thinking was that the church should constitute a sort of source of attraction, and in addition it should bring about a redesign of the urban plan of the new city within its area of influence. A remodeling of the streets, the creation of avenues, an extension of the open spaces around the new church — all were the prime objective of Gaudí's search for a monumental design.

As far as a program went, the type of church proposed started off with a model of the Gothic ground plan for a basilica, with five naves, a transept and a wide apse, with the peculiarity that the entire building was surrounded by an ambulatory, which was to be called the cloister, even though this was a rather strange version of this type of space, which is meant to be organized around an empty space and not precisely around the mass of a cathedral.

However, the most eye-catching aspect of Gaudí's concept was undoubtedly the vertical development proposed for the church. Eighteen pointed towers were to surround the structure, linked by the system of naves and exterior spaces. Taking up once more a theme characteristic of all his work — an interest in vertical elements and spaces — Gaudí proposed for the Sagrada Família an authentic apotheosis of pinnacles and towers of an imposing height, conceived undoubtedly as challenging beacons that were to soar far above the uniform landscape of terraces and roofs of the city.

Church of the Sagrada Família, Barcelona. Cross-section of the naves. c. 1914.

Yet the program for the church was also a complex iconological one, in which the cathedral was seen as part of a complicated system of symbols as well as a visual explanation of the mysteries of the faith.

At that time Gaudí was taking part in the general movement of the European Catholic world in favor of a renovation of the liturgy, for which there were in Catalonia numerous supporters and students. To re-create the language of the symbolic forms, so as to revitalize the communication that could be offered by religious objects — this was the end pursued. And so it was to be in the new church of the Sagrada Família. What happened in this case was that both in the use of symbols and in the proposal for a new liturgical organization for the Church, Gaudí demonstrated his accumulative sensitivity, which was both complex and excessive. The iconographic program for the Sagrada Família was an enormously diversified system of numbers, ciphers and symbols, expressing a multitude of doctrines that were but little used in Catholic teachings of the time. The three façades of the church were representations of the three culminating moments of the life of Christ and of the Church: birth, death and resurrection. The pointed towers were the symbolism of the exaltation of the twelve apostles, the four evangelists, the Virgin Mary and Christ himself, symbolized by the central and highest pinnacle. The lateral chapels were the symbol of baptism and of penitence, of the theological virtues and of the sorrows and joys of the patriarch, St. Joseph.

But the use of allegory and of symbols is not evoked merely by the global conception of the building. The fascination that is now exercised on us by the portions constructed by Gaudí is brought about by the multitude of allusions at all levels. Geometrical symbols, animals and plants, figures in relief or in sculpture — all of these form part of a vertiginous panorama that passes before the astonished gaze of anyone who approaches this complex edifice, conceived as an immense catechism that can speak.

In this regard it is worth noting that the level of study of the technical rationale, which so preoccupied Gaudí, is no more than the first rung of the overall concept of the building, in which, as in some microscopic vision, the animate and the inanimate join only to unfold as in a permanent discourse.

The technical-constructive willpower that Gaudí had to develop for such buildings is recalled here, as a distinct and finally dominating objective, that is to say, allegory. All the figurative reality of the fabric of the church was to be an explanation and an echo of a vision of the natural and supernatural order of things, which Gaudí wished to propound on the basis of Catholicism. However, these considerations should not conceal another aspect characteristic of the process of definition of this edifice, which is transformation in time. Given that his project came into being from the beginning as a transformation, in reality the architectural project of the Sagrada Família was at any given moment being subjected to a permanent review.

Certainly Gaudí thought that this church would summarize the whole of the research and findings of his entire career as an architect. In the classical manner, he thought that the architecture of the

Facsimile of one of Gaudí's drawings made by J. Matamala, showing the arrangement of the future Glory Façade of the Church of the Sagrada Família.

church was the culmination of the monumental style, and furthermore, the final synthesis of everything architectural. With a clear distancing from modern architecture, which arose from a thematic indifference to architectural problems, and thinking that there was a single code for composition and aesthetics that could handle any problem — from the drawing board to the city — for Gaudí, on the other hand, the church and its architecture continued to be a summary of all his experience and the site on which technical or geometrical findings were to be surpassed by a transcendent conception of this work of art.

For this reason it is not easy in the case of the Sagrada Família to separate his technical and stylistic elaboration from the total objective of the building, which puts together and transcends particular problems.

In any case, this work, which was to continue long after his death, shows very clearly the stages of maturing that took place during Gaudí's life and that we have been analyzing throughout these pages.

During the first period, from 1883 to 1893, Gaudí introduced changes in planning that foreshadowed the blossoming of the idea. But in his working on the continuation of the crypt, commenced by del Villar, and the beginning of the apse, he showed himself cautious in his use of the Gothic repertoire, which he still did not dare to criticize openly, and in which he merely introduced surprising changes, by way of ornaments of a naturalistic type.

From 1891 until approximately 1900, Gaudí worked on the construction of the Nativity Façade. Just as with the eclectic experimenting of that time on other buildings, the dominating characteristic of this part of the church is profusion. The redesign of the Gothic elements in the interior elevation and Gaudí's experiments with ornamentation, sculpture and symbolism on the exterior part of the façade seem to indicate to us the sort of preoccupation that inspired the architect at this time.

The years that we have called those of the synthesis of *Modernisme* correspond in his work to his overall definition of a building. These were the years of the first decade of the 20th century, during which a greater geometrical abstraction, a determined exploration of curved surfaces and, in general, a free and uninhibited use of any style, allowed him to make just as great an advance in his overall definition of the project, his first drawings of which were published in 1905, as in his structural handling of the solutions of the roof of the church and of the towers.

The process of reappraisal and reelaboration of Gothic architecture that we have mentioned in commenting on the project for the church of Colònia Güell came to fulfilment in the detailed study of the cross-section of the church. An initial estrangement from textbook Gothic led first of all to a naturalism of plantlike type, in which it was possible to assume in a flexible form the technical reasoning of structural continuity between arches and columns, the inclination of the supports and, in general, the three-dimensional deployment of structural arborescence.

First general view of the Church of the Sagrada Família, after a drawing done in 1906 by the architect Joan Rubió i Bellver, Gaudí's assistant.

For all that, it was not to be a satisfactory time for Gaudí, who, during the last period of his life, when he was absorbed almost totally in the problems of this work, would come back time and time again to seek solutions that were geometrically more purified, yet clearly more abstract and brutal.

The return to essentials that can be detected in his final works appears with all its force in the last surviving studies, and in the many ideas in the process of being worked out that still remained on his desk at the time of his death.

The sudden cutting-off of Gaudí's life is, in this way, a symbol of the fate of all his work, and in a very particular way of that unfinished work that is the Sagrada Família.

Gaudí's work finished brusquely and suddenly, but it bore in its own origin the cause of its lack of viability, which does not diminish his grandeur by one iota.

It is surprising to find that those who consider themselves to be the direct heirs of Gaudí have hoped to show that continuity of his teachings was possible, and have tried to create a genuine school based on the master's work, accepting what may well be one of the hypotheses in his ideas that can most readily be given a date. The materialist positivism of the 19th century put forward an idea, according to which constructive rationalism in architecture was the road by which one arrived at full artistic creativity. However, this concept brings with it the limitation that one must submit artistic creation to the narrow limits imposed by building, and further, to a method of building conceived on the basis of traditional materials and traditional systems of using them, in terms of their resistance to compression.

Fortunately Gaudí never stopped at the level of these problems, and he fashioned a creative and imaginative concept of architecture, in terms of his time, with the romantic confidence of an individual genius, and with the subjectivism appropriate to a century that made experiment a pathway to creativity and permanent change.

It is useless to recall that the cathedrals of former times were built over a period of centuries, when building methods and the anonymity of the builders introduced no changes from generation to generation. Yet today, despite a much greater discipline than in the past, when Gothic buildings were finished with baroque altarpieces and porches, we find ourselves in a situation of change in which the disappearance of the architect of a building often proves an irremediable loss. Continuation of the Sagrada Família by the successors of Gaudí assumes at the very least a lack of understanding of the conceptual changes that our times have brought about in architecture, and that, for better or for worse, connect works intimately with the genius of their authors.

The architectural adventure of Gaudí is fundamentally a personal and even autobiographical one, though he relied on a substantial number of assistants, craftsmen and artists who made the splendor of his works possible.

Yet in another way, his work, impressive and singular though it is, was built during the complex decline of the 19th-century dream of creating a new style for the society of that time by means of an architecture that would still be the offspring of ancient monumental styles. There are too many contradictions to permit one to think of Gaudí as the first modern architect and a founder of the new rationalism of our era.

On the contrary, what the work of Gaudí reveals to us, in its declining grandeur, is the permanent effort he made to understand himself and to understand the place and the time in which he lived.

The fact that the work of Gaudí is contradictory, not even permitting of confident apprentices to succeed him, is in the last analysis the explanation of his intense pathos and of his hesitant humanity.

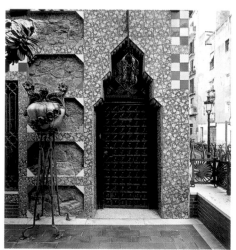

This house was built for Manuel Vicens Montaner on
Carrer de les Carolines, in the Gràcia quarter of Barcelona,
from 1883 to 1885. An addition to the building was
completed in 1925 by the architect J. B. Serra Martínez;
the garden was later destroyed when a house was
constructed next door.

Built from 1883 to 1885, this villa for Máximo Díaz de Quijano was located near the palace of the Marquis de Comillas. The work was overseen by Gaudí's assistant, Cristóbal Cascante.

The Güell family owned a large country house on the
outskirts of Barcelona, in what is now the quarter
called Les Corts. In 1883 the family commissioned Gaudí
to design a wall and gates for the property, as well as
two buildings, intended to be used as a porter's lodge
and stables, located at the main entrance.

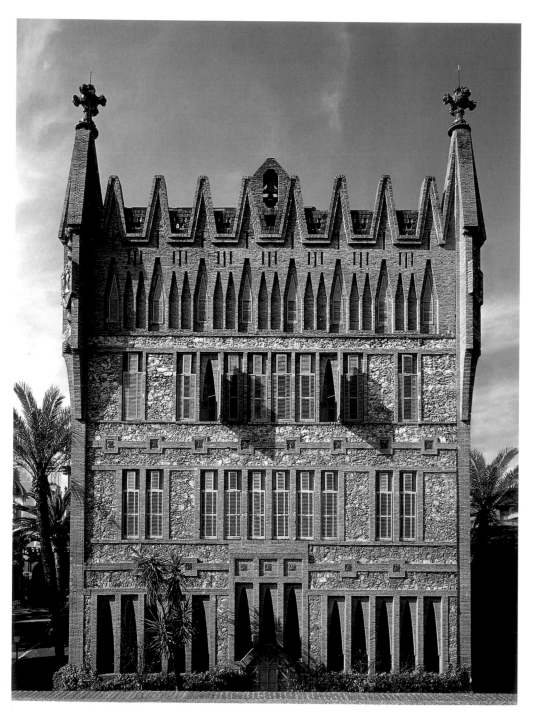

This building, constructed on a modest budget and completed in 1890, was a school and residence for the Congregation of Teresian Nuns in the Sant Gervasi quarter of Barcelona.

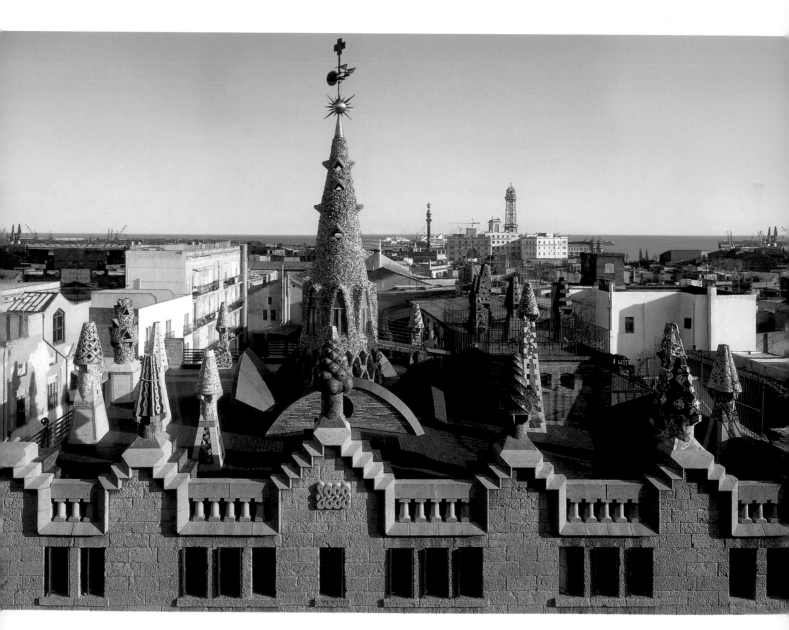

Built from 1886 to 1890 on Carrer Nou de la Rambla in Barcelona, this mansion occupied a site that had held three old houses. It was made up of six different levels, from the basement — intended for carriages — to the upper story under the roof, with its phantasmagorical forest of chimneys in whimsical forms and colors.

Bishop J. B. Grau commissioned this new episcopal palace from Gaudí in 1887. The architect was dismissed as director of works in 1893, and the building would not be completed until the second decade of the 20th century, with modifications, especially to the roof, by the new director.

This large building in the center of the city of León,
approximately rectangular in form, was designed as the main
residence of its owners and also included rental apartments.

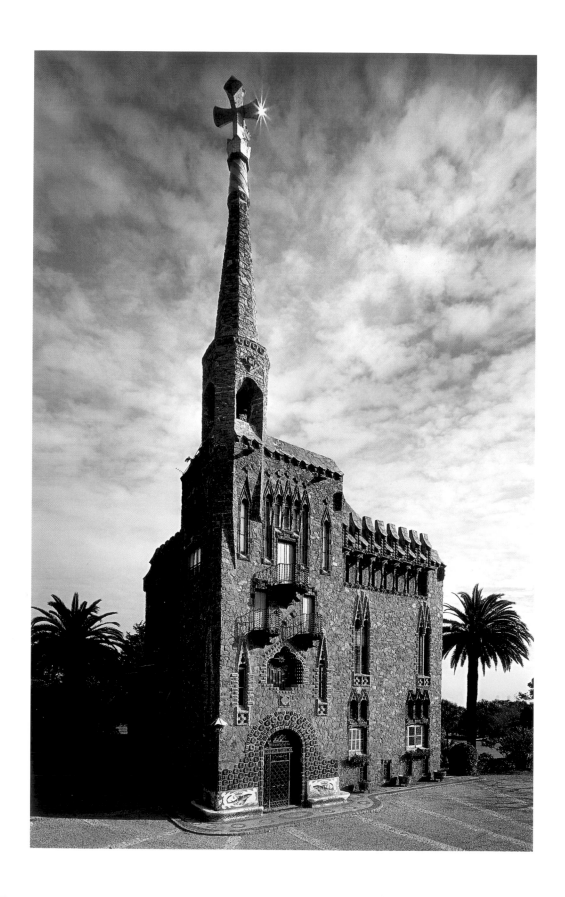

This building, designed by Gaudí for the Figueras family, was erected on a site, overlooking the plain of Barcelona, where King Martin I ("the Humane") had built a small country retreat in the 15th century. Construction was completed in 1903, and minor alterations were introduced at a later date by Gaudí's assistant Domènec Sugranyes.

In 1898 Pere Màrtir Calvet commissioned the building of an apartment block in the heart of Barcelona's Eixample; it was completed in 1900. Here Gaudí faced for the first time the problem of designing a city apartment block, an urban building type that, due to site and planning restrictions, had been characterized by extremely standardized structures. Rather than rely on preexisting solutions in approaching this building type, Gaudí explored the full range of architectural possibilities.

90

In 1904 Josep Batlló Casanova commissioned additions and renovations to the house on his property on Passeig de Gràcia in Barcelona. Just as work was beginning, a house designed by the architect Puig i Cadafalch was completed next door. In his work on Casa Batlló, Gaudí collaborated with several assistants; the most distinctive contributions were made by Josep Maria Jujol in the ornamentation and use of color.

Eusebi Güell, Gaudí's patron and protector, was interested in creating a residential park, both as a speculative investment (he intended to sell off plots of land) and as a trial of the utopian garden city, of which he was a strong advocate. Although Park Güell was to become a disaster from an economic standpoint, Gaudí's work on the overall plan, circulation, and general services allowed him to explore his ideas for a suburban residential area and the architecture needed to serve it. Work continued from 1900 to 1914.

The largest apartment building Gaudí built in the Eixample of Barcelona was this complex on Passeig de Gràcia, financed by the Milà family in 1906 and completed in 1910. The unusual nature of the complex's massive stone façades led to the nickname "La Pedrera" (stone quarry). Although housing blocks — typically with beveled corners — were common in the Eixample, Gaudí eschewed traditional treatments in favor of completely original spatial and structural solutions.

In 1904 Gaudí undertook the restoration of this cathedral, a Gothic building in the Catalan tradition that was highly valued by Gothic specialists of the time. The project consisted of removing the choir from the central nave and moving the stalls to the chancel. By designing new pulpits, canopies, lamps and choir stalls with deliriously colored floral ornamentation, Gaudí effected a complete reappraisal of the preexisting Gothic space.

Although it has not been proven with certainty, it seems very likely that these drawings depict the commission Gaudí worked on in 1908 for a great skyscraper hotel intended for New York City. The only remaining evidence of this project is the drawings made in the 1950s by the sculptor J. Matamala, a faithful disciple and assistant of Gaudí, who attempted to recall and reconstitute the master's intentions.

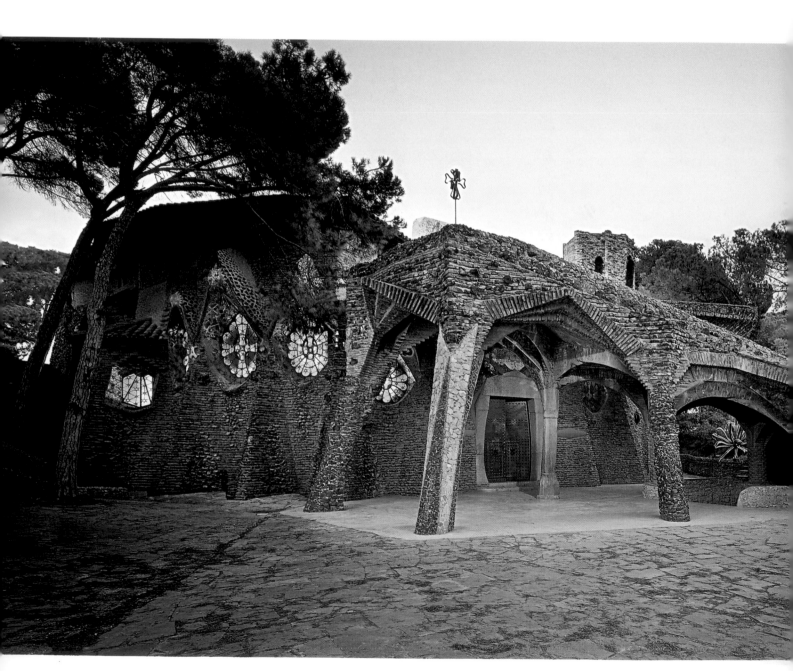

The Güell family had organized one of the first industrial settlements in Spain, transferring their textile industry from the outskirts of Barcelona to the village of Santa Coloma de Cervelló. Although Gaudí and his assistants were also involved in designing other parts of the workers' colony, their most compelling work was on the church.

Dominating the site from a low hill, the church was meant to preside over the complex of the new township. Gaudí started work on the plan in 1890, although building did not begin until 1908. Construction was halted in 1915, by which time only the crypt had been completed.

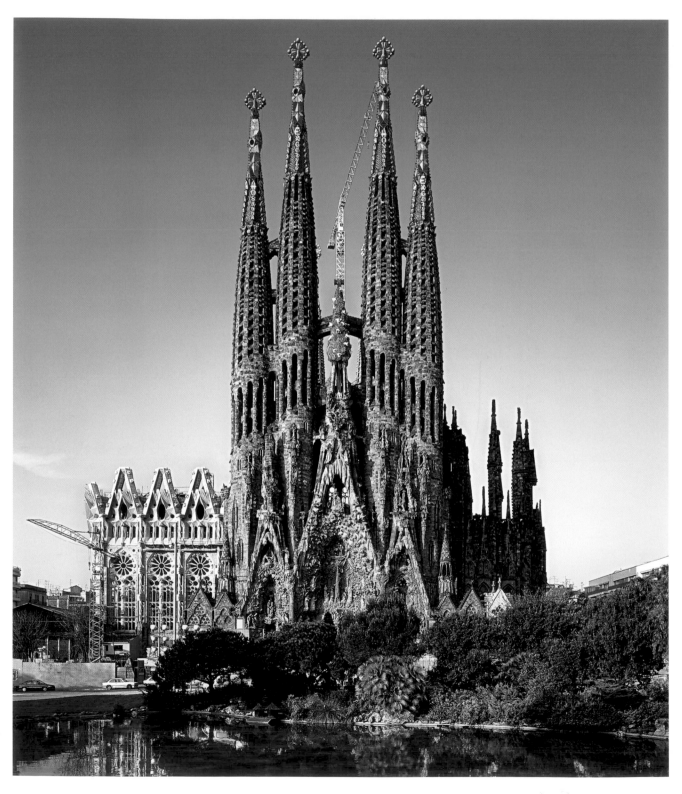

134

The work on the Sagrada Família was begun by the architect Francisco de Paula del Villar in 1882, and Gaudí took over the commission in 1884. It would occupy him until his death in 1926. Conceived as a new cathedral for the new city of Barcelona, the project underwent many modifications throughout the architect's lifetime. The various stylistic stages of Gaudí's work can be recognized in the evolution of the cathedral; even its unfinished condition is a clear expression of his ambitious ideas about monumental architecture. The church, the sum total of his architectural concerns, was conceived as an experiment in synthesizing the structural, the symbolic and the monumental.

CHRONOLOGICAL SUMMARY

1852. Antoni Gaudí i Cornet is born in Reus on June 25.

1873–78. He begins his studies at the School of Architecture in Barcelona, obtaining his degree on March 15, 1878. During these years, he works with the architects Joan Martorell and Francisco de Paula del Villar, and with the building supervisor, Josep Fontserè.

1878. Lampposts for Plaça Reial in Barcelona.

Housing units and workshops for the Workers' Cooperative in Mataró, Barcelona.

1881. Project for the Sea Wall in Barcelona. Not built.

1882. Project for warehouses for Eusebi Güell, in Garraf, Barcelona. Not built.

1883. Apartment house for Manuel Vicens in Carrer de les Carolines, Barcelona.

House for the Marquis de Comillas, in Comillas, Santander, known as "El Capricho."

1884. He receives the commission to continue work on the Expiatory Church of the Sagrada Família, commenced by the architect Francisco de Paula del Villar.

Stables in Les Corts in Barcelona, for Güell.

1886. Palace for Eusebi Güell in Carrer Nou de la Rambla in Barcelona.

1887. Episcopal Palace of Astorga in León.

1888. Teresian Convent School in Barcelona.

1890. Work begins on Colònia Güell in Santa Coloma de Cervelló, near Barcelona.

1891. "Casa de los Botines" in León.

1892. Project for the Catholic Missions in Tangier. Not built.

1898. Casa Calvet in Carrer de Casp, Barcelona.

1900. Country house, Torre Bellesguard, in Barcelona.

Work begins on Park Güell on the Muntanya Pelada in Barcelona.

1904. Alterations to the cathedral of Palma de Mallorca.

Renovation of Casa Batlló on Passeig de Gràcia in Barcelona.

1906. Casa Milà ("La Pedrera") in Barcelona.

1908. Project for a hotel in New York. Not built.

1926. Gaudí dies on June 10 in Hospital de la Santa Creu, in Barcelona, after being knocked down by a tramcar.

SELECTED BIBLIOGRAPHY

A+U Architecture and Urbanism (Nakamura, Tokyo, 1977), no. 86 (issue devoted to Gaudí).

BASSEGODA NONELL, Juan. *Antonio Gaudí. Vida y Arquitectura.* Barcelona-Tarragona, 1977.

    Gaudí. Salvat, Barcelona, 1987.

    La Pedrera de Gaudí. Caixa de Catalunya, Barcelona, 1987.

    El gran Gaudí. Ausa, Sabadell, 1989.

BERGÓS I MASSÓ, Joan. *Gaudí, el hombre y la obra.* Universitat Politènica de Catalunya, Barcelona, 1974.

BERGÓ I MASSÓ, Joan; Marc LLIMARGAS I CASAS. *Gaudí: el hombre y la obra.* Círculo de Lectores, Barcelona, 2002.

BOHIGAS, Oriol. *Arquitectura Modernista.* Lumen, Barcelona, 1968.

CASANELLAS, Enric. *Nueva visión de Gaudí.* Polígrafa, Barcelona, 1964.

CIRICI I PELLICER, Alexandre. *El arte modernista catalán.* Ayma, Barcelona, 1951.

CIRLOT, Juan-Eduardo. *El arte de Gaudí.* Omega, Barcelona, 1965.

COLLINS, George R. *Antonio Gaudí.* G. Braziller, New York, 1960.

    Bibliography of Antonio Gaudí and the Catalan Movement 1870-1930. Charlottersville, 1973.

FLORES LÓPEZ, Carlos. *Gaudí, Jujol y el modernismo catalán.* Aguilar, Madrid, 1982.

    Introducción a Gaudí. Aguilar, Madrid, 1983.

    La lección de Gaudí. Espasa-Calpe, Madrid, 2002.

GIRALT-MIRACLE, Daniel, and others. *Gaudí 2002. Any Internacional Gaudí. Miscel·lània.* Planeta – Ajuntament de Barcelona, 2002.

    Gaudí, la búsqueda de la forma: espacio, geometría, estructura y construcción. Lunwerg Editores, Barcelona, 2002.

GÜELL, X. *Antoni Gaudí.* Gustavo Gili, Barcelona, 1987.

LAHUERTA, Juan José, and others. *Gaudí i el seu temps.* Barcanova, Barcelona, 1990.

MARTINELL, César. *Gaudinismo.* Amigos de Gaudí, Barcelona, 1954.

    Gaudí: su vida, su teoría, su obra. Collegi Oficial d'Arquitectes de Catalunya, Barcelona, 1967.

    Antoni Gaudí, arquitecte. Ajuntament de Barcelona, 1977.

PANE, Roberto. *Gaudí.* Edizioni di Comunità, Milan, 1964, 1982[2].

PERMANYER, Lluís. *Història de l'Eixample.* Plaza y Janés, Barcelona, 1991.

    El Gaudí de Barcelona. Polígrafa, Barcelona, 1996.

    Un paseo por la Barcelona Modernista. Polígrafa, Barcelona, 1998.

PERUCHO, Joan. *Gaudí, una arquitectura de anticipación.* Polígrafa, Barcelona, 1967.

PEVSNER, Nikolaus. «The strange architecture di Antonio Gaudí», in *The Lister*, no. 7, August 1952.

PUJOLS, Francesc; Salvador DALÍ; Robert DESCHARNES; Clovis PREVOST. *La visió artística i religiosa de Gaudí.* Aymà, Barcelona, 1949.

RÀFOLS, Josep Frances; Francesc FOLGUERA. *Gaudí.* Canosa, Barcelona, 1929.

RAMÍREZ, Juan Antonio. *Gaudí.* Grupo Anaya, Madrid, 1992.

SERT, Josep Lluís. *Cripta de la Colònia Güell de Antoni Gaudí.* Polígrafa, Barcelona, 1968.

SOLÀ-MORALES, Ignasi de. *Gaudí.* Polígrafa, Barcelona, 1983.

SWEENEY, J. J.; Josep Lluís SERT. *Antoni Gaudí.* Architectural Press, London, 1960.

TANAKA, Hiroya. *Metodología gráfica, dibujos y proporciones de la obra de Gaudí.* Universitat Politècnica de Catalunya, Barcelona, 1993.

TARRAGÓ, Salvador. *Gaudí.* El Escudo de Oro, Barcelona, 1998.

ZEVI, Bruno. «Un genio catalano: Antonio Gaudí», in *Metron* (Rome), no. 38, 1950.